To John, Greg, and Jane

Contents

✒ Preface

In editing the book reviews in this collection, I have been careful to preserve Katherine Anne Porter's intentions as far as I have been able to determine them. I have made no effort to alter her grammar or change her spelling, even in the interest of consistency, unless I have concluded to the best of my ability that an error, typographical or other, was made by the original editor or the printer. In such cases I have made necessary corrections silently. In doubtful instances, I have let the original text stand.

One of the distinguishing features of Porter's style is her habit of using within her prose a series of periods, varying in number. Although such a series may look like ellipses, it is not. She also used the colon in imaginative ways, in places other writers might have used the semicolon. Such practices are integral parts of her style and in fact often delineate refinements of meaning.

I have made uniform the designation of titles of published works. Because most of the original reviews were set in type that did not include italics, book titles were commonly placed in quotation marks. I have changed them to italics throughout the reviews. In the Introduction I have not tried to differentiate among Porter's short stories, long stories, and short novels with the use of italics, preferring to indicate with quotation marks the titles of all her individual fictional works except *Ship of Fools.*

I wish to thank the University of Nevada, Las Vegas, for various kinds of institutional support of this project.

✍ Introduction

Between 1920 and 1958 Katherine Anne Porter published more than sixty-five book reviews and several times provided a list of her favorite books for a given year. Most of the reviews were written for much-needed money, but occasionally she reviewed friends' books as a favor. In 1952 she chose twelve of her published reviews to be reprinted in *The Days Before,* a collection of her personal and critical essays, and in 1970 she added seven more to those twelve for reprinting in *The Collected Essays and Occasional Writings of Katherine Anne Porter.*[1] Before her last illness she had planned to gather and publish most of the remaining reviews.

With the exception of those in *The Collected Essays and Occasional Writings,* Porter's reviews have not been readily accessible. Many were published in the *New York Herald Tribune* and have been available to most people only on microfilm. Others, which appeared for the most part in the *New York Times,* the *New Republic,* the *Nation,* and *New Masses,* have had to be individually retrieved.

A comparison of Porter's early and late reviews shows no discernible difference in style and reveals no substantial change in her social values or artistic standards. If some of the reviews are more critically weighty than others, almost all give some insight into Porter and her art. Many of the reviews reveal Porter's public positions on political, religious, and social issues, which in turn are relevant to the fiction. The reviews also reflect the themes that dominate her fiction. Many reviews contain statements about Porter's concept of art and her view of the role of the artist. Collectively the reviews define, implicitly and explicitly, the critical apparatus that Porter applied to others' works and that underlies the aesthetic assumptions in her own fiction.

Katherine Anne Porter was born Callie Russell Porter in 1890 in Indian Creek, Texas, the fourth child of Harrison Boone Porter and Mary Alice Jones Porter. After the death of her mother in 1892, Callie and her surviving sisters and brother were reared by their father and his widowed mother, Catherine Anne Skaggs Porter, in Kyle, Texas. Although the family was poor and Callie's formal education was scant, consisting of erratic country schooling and a year at a private school, she revealed an early appreciation for literature and drama that was nurtured by books (classics preserved from a more affluent family past or borrowed from neighbors and friends), family legends, and a family reverence for language.

When Callie was sixteen she married John Henry Koontz, a railroad clerk and a member of a prosperous south Texas family. Several years after the marriage, she converted to Roman Catholicism, her husband's religion. The marriage, however, was barren and unhappy, and after seven years Callie left her husband and Texas. She went to Chicago to try to earn a living in the movies. With the subsequent divorce in 1915, Callie Russell changed her name to Katherine Anne. Her health failed at the same time her acting ambitions and her marriage ended, and she spent a dark and horrible period in Dallas and Carlsbad, Texas, hospitals recovering from tuberculosis. Her emergence from her illness marked the modest beginning of her writing career.

Porter's early writing experience was as a journalist, first for the Fort Worth *Critic* and later for the *Rocky Mountain News* in Denver, where she reviewed movies, plays, and vaudeville—important preparation for her later book reviewing as well as her fiction writing. Her ever-fragile health made her a ready victim of the 1918 influenza epidemic, and the Denver years were marked by her second brush with death, which would form the surface material for her short novel "Pale Horse, Pale Rider" (1937). After she regained her health this second time, Porter left Denver and went to New York City.

While she was living in Greenwich Village among writers, artists, and intellectuals, Porter supported herself by writing publicity releases for a motion picture company, rewriting children's stories that were based on well-known fables, and ghostwriting a young American woman's account of marriage to a Chinese student (*My Chinese Marriage*).[2] She became acquainted with several Mexican artists, among them Tato Nacho and Adolpho Best-Maugard, who made possible a magazine assignment to Mexico, where there was "a terribly exciting" revolution going on, one that she "ran smack into," she told an interviewer years later.[3]

Having grown up in Texas, Porter was familiar with Mexico. She spoke a little Spanish and had known Mexicans and Mexican-Americans in Texas. A trip deep into Mexico to Mexico City in 1920, however, opened her eyes to a larger perspective, and she was soon caught up in the excitement of the current Mexican revolution, a cultural and political upheaval that idealistically aimed, as had many previous revolutions in Mexico, to obliterate Mexico's caste system and restore Mexico to its purer past. A natural outgrowth of such an intention was a renewed interest in Mexico's ruins and its primitive art forms. Soon after her arrival in Mexico City, Porter met William Niven, an aged archaeologist, and Manuel Gamio, a distinguished anthropologist and the director of the archaeological division of the national museum. Her friendship with Nacho, Best-Maugard, and other Mexican artists in Greenwich Village gave her immediate entrée to the large circle of revolutionary artists, many of them muralists, who were credited with providing the impetus for the revolution. The group included Xavier Guerrero, Carlos Merida, Jorge Encisco, and the eighteen-year-old Miguel Covarrubias. The most important figure in the movement was Diego Rivera, with whom Porter became well acquainted.

While Porter was absorbing the excitement of the revolution, she was intelligently analyzing the state of affairs in the place she called her "second country." In 1920 she herself had idealistic hopes for the revolution's success, as her letters to family and friends attest. She became a staff member and for a short period editor of the English-language section of *El Heraldo de Mexico*, dabbled in revolutionary activity, joined a feminist organization, and for a time espoused socialist and communist beliefs. But Porter was not by nature idealistic, and amazingly soon she was able to see serious problems in the leadership and ideology of the revolution, problems she discussed in articles written in 1921 and 1922 for the *Century* and the *Freeman*.[4] She addressed the same problems obliquely in her first stories: "María Concepción" (1922), in which she depicted the difficulty of "civilizing" the Indian; "The Martyr" (1923), in which she illustrated the Mexican proclivity for an impractical romanticism; and "Virgin Violeta" (1924), in which she illustrated the Catholic church's disservice in encouraging paternalism and an unrealistic view of love. By the end of the decade, in her stories "Flowering Judas" (1930), "Hacienda" (1932), and "That Tree" (1934), Porter was able to trace the complicated causes of what she regarded as the revolution's failure.

If Porter lost her hope for the revolution's success, she did not lose her appreciation for either the Mexican people or primitive art. In 1921 she wrote a pamphlet, *Outline of Mexican Popular Arts and Crafts*,[5] which was to accompany an exhibit to the United States, and in 1924 she wrote an appreciative article on the *corrido*, a form of Mexican folk ballad.[6] In 1925 she published the first of her studies of Diego Rivera and his work.[7] Steeped in Mexico's cultural past and involved for a time in Mexico's revolutionary present, Porter was considered by many to be an articulate authority on Mexican affairs.

Porter's Mexico years (1920–1931) were in fact broken up by long stays in the United States and Bermuda that included the beginning and end of her second marriage. Although the time she spent outside Mexico during those eleven years was cumulatively longer than the total time she spent in Mexico, the Mexican experience was profoundly important to Porter's art, second only to her family experience in Texas. During the 1920s, when Porter began to write and publish fiction based on her experiences in Mexico, her previously half-formed worldview and aesthetic theories began to crystallize.

Porter's income from her early published stories was small, and she gladly accepted offers to review books for the *New York Herald Tribune* and the *New Republic*. Although she accepted money from friends as loans or gifts and from publishers as advances, during the 1920s most of her earned income derived from reviewing. By the time her first collection of stories, *Flowering Judas*, appeared in 1930, Porter had published only nine separate stories, but she had published more than thirty-five book reviews. Her first voyage to Europe in 1931 was made possible by a Guggenheim Fellowship, and, for whatever reasons, while she was in Europe she published no reviews.

The decision to stop reviewing books held firm until 1936, when Porter reviewed Carleton Beals's *The Stones Awake: A Novel of Mexico* for the *New Republic*. In 1937 she published four reviews and began doing book reviews for the *Nation* as well as for the *New York Herald Tribune* and the *New Republic*. By this time Porter's small but substantial critical reputation, her travels in Europe, her familiarity with Mexico, her opinions on women writers and feminist issues, and her own wide-ranging knowledge made her a respected and prized reviewer. But in 1938 Porter again took a break from reviewing books. She dissolved her third marriage—to Eugene Pressly, whom she had married in 1933—and married Albert Erskine, her fourth and last husband. She divorced him in 1942.

During Porter's marriage to Erskine, she lived most of the time in Louisiana. Income from her fiction had accelerated modestly with the reprinting of *Flowering Judas and Other Stories* by the Modern Library and the appearance in 1938 of *Pale Horse, Pale Rider: Three Short Novels*. Her third collection, *The Leaning Tower and Other Stories* (1944), enlarged her already considerable literary reputation and brought in a steady but small income, which she supplemented with advances from publishers who were eager for more collections of her stories as well as the projected long novel. From 1941 to 1949 Porter published only six reviews. In 1950 she approached her earlier reviewing activity with six reviews, but by then she had become even more selective in the books she agreed to review, taking books only by friends or books about which she held especially strong opinions. Six reviews appeared irregularly between 1951 and 1958. Her finances improved dramatically for short periods in 1945 and 1946 when she went to Hollywood to work as a scriptwriter. She gave up the lucrative job twice when it was apparent to her that her own fiction writing was suffering. After she began to accept university

appointments in 1948, she again had less need for the extra money
the reviews brought in, but at this time she did agree to review a few
books for the *New York Times*. Several times she identified "Books
I Have Liked" for the *New York Herald Tribune* and supplied to the
New York Times her list of the best books of the year.[8] Porter published no book reviews during the several years in which she was
trying to finish her only long novel, *Ship of Fools*. After its publica-
tion in 1962 she finally did not need the money at all, and she had
lost interest in reviewing friends' works or in using the book review
as a forum to set the record straight or to present a case for art.

When Porter died in Washington, D.C., in 1980 at the age of ninety,
she left behind a unified body of both fiction and nonfiction that remains exemplary in its quality. Her words in the preface to the first
collection of her nonfiction, *The Days Before* (1952), remind us of the
contribution of her book reviews, as well as her essays and poetry,
to the understanding of the philosophical and aesthetic values that
inform her fiction. Referring to the relationship between her fiction
and nonfiction, she said, "It is all one thing. The two ways of working helped and supported each other. I needed both." She expressed
the hope that readers of her nonfiction would find there "the shape,
direction, and connective tissue of a continuous, central interest and
preoccupation of a lifetime."[9]

While Porter accurately pointed out a relationship between her fiction and nonfiction, important differences are also apparent. Porter
spoke with several different narrative and personal voices. There is a
narrative voice in her fiction that differs subtly from the voice of her
nonfiction; a still different voice appears in the spontaneous inter-
views she gave; and additional voices emerge in her letters and the
marginalia of the books she owned. In the fiction the persona is detached, truthful, and ironic. In the nonfiction the persona is more
emotional: indignant (sometimes angry), nostalgic, and admiring;
but the emotion is tempered with a reasonable and moral tone. The
views expressed in her letters and the marginal comments in her
many books show that her private opinions, uttered impulsively and
subject to change, sometimes were at odds with her public voice.

Of the more than seventy-five books Porter reviewed, many fall
into areas of Porter's recognized interests and expertise. Of those in
this collection and in *The Collected Essays and Occasional Writings*,
in overlapping categories, seventeen are books about Mexico
and thirty-five are books by or about women. Ten books she reviewed were written by travel writers or explorers, and four books
have Puritan subjects. Miscellaneous books include biographies of
Daniel Boone, Laurence Sterne, Cotton Mather, and Louis XI; essays
by E. M. Forster and Max Beerbohm; a study of medieval life; novels
by W. L. George, François Boyer, William Goyen, John Cooper Powys,
and Glenway Wescott; a picture book of New Orleans; three works
by or about Dylan Thomas; and the collected letters of Ezra Pound.

Porter's first published reviews appeared in *El Heraldo de Mexico*
soon after her arrival in Mexico City. In the November 22, 1920,
issue her angry review of *Mexico in Revolution*, by Blasco Ibañez,
appeared, and the following month she reviewed W. L. George's *Caliban*, Jeanette Lee's *The Chinese Coat*, and Leonard Merrick's *The
House of Lynch* (December 15, 1920). Her first review in an American newspaper was a consideration of two books on Mexico: Harry L.
Foster's *A Gringo in Mañanaland* and Vernon Quinn's *Beautiful
Mexico*. Porter already had written *Outline of Mexican Popular Arts
and Crafts*, for which she had done significant research, and in these
reviews she quoted again some of her sources for that earlier work.
It is apparent that Porter was dismayed at what was then being published about Mexico, referring to the "growing rubbish heap which
is literature about Mexico," which must have included the book by
Ibañez she had reviewed for *El Heraldo*. She complained in a letter
to Genevieve Taggard that reviewing wearied her, especially since
she seemed to be sent every bad book written on Mexico.[10] Although
she praised Foster for having no political message to deliver—a standard to which she adhered and held others all her life—and Quinn
for his careful restatement of the main points of Mexican history,
she found more to condemn in the two books than to admire. She
attacked Foster for his too-easy goodwill and superficiality, and she
attacked Quinn for his materialism and obvious feeling of American

superiority—traits she attached to particular characters in "Hacienda," "That Tree," and *Ship of Fools.*

Porter charged other writers of books on Mexico with related faults. In "Paternalism and the Mexican Problem" Porter said that the authors of *Some Mexican Problems* and *Aspects of Mexican Civilization,* three of whom were friends of hers, had been too optimistic about Mexico and too kind to Mexico's internal enemies.[11] In 1943 she took Anita Brenner to task for having been too gentle with "individual villains" in her book *The Wind That Swept Mexico* ("Mexico's Thirty Long Years of Revolution") and for failing to expose the oil companies that exploited Mexico's natural wealth. Porter, however, greatly admired Brenner's earlier *Idols Behind Altars* ("Old Gods and New Messiahs"), which she had judged "a book about Mexico not to be missed—a stimulating record of a vital period in the history of American art." Porter's review of *Idols Behind Altars* is important for what it reveals about aspects of the ancient culture that Porter dealt with in her fiction. Porter said that Brenner investigated "the precise nature of the Aztec idol which lies under the Catholic altars" in order to trace "an inner spiritual unity" between the ancient Indians and the current revolution. In "María Concepción" Porter had addressed the superimposition of Catholicism on the primitive religions of the Indians, but she had depicted in that story not unity but conflict between the old and the new, with the primitive ways ultimately proving stronger. In "Flowering Judas" and "Hacienda" she linked the phenomenon more directly to the revolution, but one of her canonical themes came to be the connection between surface appearance and the inner reality. Porter no doubt drew reinforcement, if not inspiration, from points Brenner made in *Idols Behind Altars.*

Porter had praised another book on the subject of Mexico's ancient past—*In an Unknown Land,* by Thomas Gann, a British archaeologist whom she may have met and with whose work she probably was familiar through Gamio. Her review ("Maya Treasure") is primarily a summary of Gann's book, which she called "a valuable pioneer work of reference to the amateur, a textbook of suggestions for further reading."

In general Porter found more to appreciate in the artistic record of Mexico than she found in what she regarded as fainthearted contemporaries' social and political analyses. Porter reviewed two collections of photographs of the paintings of Diego Rivera, the model for Rubén in Porter's early story "The Martyr" (1923). *The Frescoes of Diego Rivera*, with an introduction by Ernestine Evans, was published in 1929, and Porter was unequivocal in her praise of Rivera's contribution to modern painting: "I believe that he is the most important living painter." Eight years later, in her review of *Portrait of Mexico*, the result of a collaboration between Rivera and his biographer, Bertram Wolfe, Porter was still able to praise Rivera's achievements, although she had become disillusioned with him personally. She said that "no single man in his time has ever had more influence on the eye and mind of the public who know his work than Diego Rivera." She continued, "For myself, and I believe I speak for great numbers, Mexico does not appear to me as it did before I saw Rivera's paintings of it."

Rivera had been especially appreciative of the beauty and truth of primitivism, and Porter was quick to discern in some books on Mexico not only a failure to appreciate the Indian but also a condescension on the part of the foreign writer toward Mexico. From Porter's viewpoint, it was D. H. Lawrence's most serious failure in *The Plumed Serpent*. Porter said that Lawrence had gone to Mexico "in the hope of finding there, among alien people and their mysterious cult, what he had failed to find in his own race or within himself, a center and a meaning to life." Although she went on to say that Lawrence failed because he was incapable of seeing the real Mexico and understanding his own blood tie to the Indian, Porter was defining the lure of the primitive, which she treated in "María Concepción," "Flowering Judas," "Hacienda," and "That Tree." Porter expanded this view of primitivism to embrace the large aspect of human existence that includes death, cruelty, sexuality, and instinct, acceptance of which is central to human spiritual maturation, the related theme she explored in "The Circus," "The Grave," "Pale Horse, Pale Rider," and *Ship of Fools*.

Porter found Lawrence's kind of failure in many travel books. She was an inveterate traveler, often describing her life as nomadic. Wandering from place to place for most of her life gave her a perspective that accounts for the variety of settings in her fiction, and it also gave her an understanding of the spirit of adventure that motivated explorers and world travelers. She even said in "Shooting the Chutes" that she hoped to write a travel book herself someday. In the books she reviewed by travelers and explorers, she disliked what she had disliked in many of the books about Mexico: an inability to appreciate and respect the alien people one traveled among. She pointed out that Lafcadio Hearn, for example, never understood the Japanese he lived among ("A Disinherited Cosmopolitan"), and that Frank Hedges Butler, Harman Black, and Dorothy Dix described foreign people, especially primitive people, from a position of superiority or pity ("Shooting the Chutes"). Porter was more appreciative of Cecil Herbert Prodgers's *Adventures in Peru,* which is charming in its honesty, as she was for the same reason of Marc Lescarbot's early seventeenth-century description of Arcadia. But her greatest praise was offered to R. B. Cunninghame Graham for three of his works that Porter reviewed in 1927 ("Black, White, Red, Yellow and the Pintos"), a time when she was particularly critical of the "rubbish heap" of books on Mexico. Porter said of Graham: "He has been almost everywhere, and everything has had a meaning and an interest for him. . . . He has got acquainted with enough of each kind and color to discover their under-the-skin likenesses and differences, and he tells of them not as if they were shows put on for his special amusement, but as human creatures that need not be hated or despised, or feared, or improved." Graham's attitude toward his subjects is close to the detachment Porter consistently sought in the narrative voice of her fiction.

In addition to being something of an authority on travel and Mexican affairs, Porter was also an independent woman and something of a feminist. Consequently, book-review editors routinely sent her books written by or about women. Many of her reviews reveal her concerns about women's rights and her understanding of women's historical place in Western civilization.[12] In her short review of W. L. George's *The Story of Women* ("Mr. George on the Woman Problem"), she indicates that her own feminist sympathies were awakened in her youth, as was her animosity toward George, whose novels *Caliban* and *The Triumph of Gallio* ("A Self-Made Ghost") she already had reviewed unfavorably. "Years ago," she wrote, "when I was badly upset over the fact that women enjoyed no suffrage at the ballot box, it annoyed me grievously to hear Mr. W. L. George referred to as a friend of women; as a man who understood women, at that." Describing her younger self as "endlessly suspicious of gentlemen authors who wrote slick, patronizing articles about us for the syndicated press," she "rejected the good offices of Mr. George and repudiated his ideas about us," concluding, "Time has confirmed this adolescent judgment." She objected strongly to George's suggestion that women are a "problem," which has been ameliorated only by "the human benevolence of men."

Porter was equally direct in her 1925 review of *Our Changing Morality: A Symposium* ("Sex and Civilization"), a collection of essays by well-known people about changing sexual mores. Porter's familiar ironic tone discloses various contributors' prudishness, biases, and wrongheadedness, reserving praise only for Bertrand Russell and Edwin Muir. She bristled especially at Charlotte Perkins Gilman, who "belongs to a generation which clicks the tongue and lifts the eyebrow at the connection, even in words, of 'joy' and 'sex,' " a position she expounded upon in her essay "Marriage Is Belonging"[13] and developed thematically in "Holiday," which she wrote in the 1920s. While Porter agreed that women suffer in general from a lack of freedom and from biased social attitudes, Gilman's views of women as victims and instruments of "the ranging greedy passions of men" were "incomprehensible" to Porter "in this age." Among the contributors Porter discerned two clear camps in the male and female viewpoints: "The women are more minute, realistic, explicit and urgent" than men, who are "largely content to advance by cycles of evolution." She described this perceptible pull and haul as "the difference in gait between the shod and the free foot."

Porter's disdain intensified in her review of a male-supremacist work, *Lysistrata, or Woman's Future and Future Woman*, by Anthony M. Ludovici, and *Hypatia, or Woman and Knowledge*, by Dora (Mrs. Bertrand) Russell. Porter described Ludovici as having begun "with a single idea and that a fallacy" and having "created a whole set of airy worlds with god-like nonchalance and lack of forethought." She devastatingly paraphrased his central argument: "There was a time, says the author, taking refuge in pre-historic aeons, when men were lords of life and women were their cheerful, obedient dependents. On these terms, love was ecstasy, health was perfect, there was no provoking feminist agitation or scientific tampering with the psyche." She pointed out that "of economic and political problems he says nothing, so we are happily to presume that they had not been invented." She continued in the same ironic voice: "The decline of this natural supremacy of men over women, due to the unaccountable discontent of the women themselves, whom nothing can please, has brought man low and the world to its present unhealthful state." Porter delighted in what she regarded as Dora Russell's neat demolition of Ludovici's dream world. Mrs. Russell was, Porter said, "a direct descendant of that first pre-historic virago who turned a realistic eye upon her surroundings and perceived that a man standing between her and the world represented not so much defense, protection, entertainment and nourishment as a mere shutting out of light and air."

While Porter may have identified powerfully with the viragos and independent women who had managed to find the delight of being barefoot, her feminism was rarely expressed so strongly as in those three reviews. An exception is her 1951 review of the *Short Novels of Colette*, in which she voiced indignation that a female artist should have been judged by a standard different from that for her male counterparts. This issue offended Porter the artist as well as Porter the woman. In her review of the collection, with an introduction by her friend Glenway Wescott, Porter launched an attack on the French for not giving Colette her proper place in French letters. She said that although in France Colette's work was known and loved, she was nevertheless regarded with a tone of "particular indulgence, reserved for gifted women who make no pretensions and know how to keep their place in the arts: a modest second-best, no matter how good, to the next ranking male." Wescott said that since both Proust and Gide are dead, Colette is "the greatest living French fiction writer," but Porter insisted that Colette was the greatest even while Gide and Proust lived.

Her reviews of books about women confirm repeatedly her admiration for women like herself who had flouted the traditional roles their societies had given them. Porter admired Katharine Anthony's *Catherine the Great* not only for the lucid writing and careful attention to historical accuracy, but also for the portrait of Catherine, who suffered the infamy of a paternalistic society that did not allow women the same freedoms enjoyed by men ("The Great Catherine"). She liked Anthony's translation of Catherine's memoirs ("Semiramus Was a Good Girl") for the same reasons. Porter no doubt identified with Catherine's stifling environment, her "long process of liberation," her miserable first marriage, her irrational selection of lovers, her sensitivity to the arts, and the force of her will.

In 1925 Porter reviewed *Original Letters from India (1779–1815)*, by Eliza Fay ("The Complete Letter Writer"). Porter admired Fay for being "this obdurate, tough-souled creature, who gave her squalid fate a sturdy battle," just as she grudgingly admired Rosalie Caden Evans ("La Conquistadora") for her extraordinary will and courage, even if misplaced. In "A Philosopher at Court" Porter reviewed *A Lady in Waiting to Queen Victoria*, memoirs edited by the daughter of Lady Ponsonby. Porter pointed out that "the ladies of the Victorian Age have been unfortunate in their legend: it is true that the best of them had decorum to excess, but they never have been sufficiently praised for their vitality." Porter admired Lady Ponsonby's intellectual vigor and independence of thought. She admired the same qualities in Hannah Whitall Smith ("A Quaker Who 'Had a Splendid Time of It' ").

When Porter reviewed *The Lost Art: Letters of Seven Famous Women* ("Not So Lost!"), she found it ironic that letter writing, "a subsidiary art" and "one of the hundred ramifications of the vast female duty to please," should have been done so well by these women who were not at all "professional pleasers." She admired their interest in daily living, their willingness to be indiscreet and frank, and their willingness to disclose their moods and thoughts to the trusted persons they addressed, in the process capturing "their own essences." The virtues that Porter identified in Catherine the Great and the traits she clearly admired in Eliza Fay, Dora Russell, Lady Ponsonby, Hannah Smith, and other women are the traits she gave to her most admirable fictional women: Miranda Gay, Sophia Jane Rhea (Miranda's grandmother), and Jenny Brown in *Ship of Fools*.

In a variety of reviews Porter attacked antifeminism incidentally but directly. She charged D. H. Lawrence with having "a grudge against women as opposed to his concept of woman,"[14] and she pointed out that Dylan Thomas, who "thought women fit only for bed and board," betrayed his wife, Caitlin, "as masculine matter of course" while demanding "the most rigid fidelity of her."[15] She was scathing in her attack on Christopher Sykes and his "monkish distrust of women,"[16] and she berated Wyndham Lewis for appearing to approve of Louis XI's acts against women ("The Most Catholic King"). Her strongest charge was leveled at H. G. Wells, who published posthumously a selection of short stories by his wife, Catherine, whom he described in terms of her complete devotion to him ("The Hundredth Role"). Porter said that Catherine Wells, a woman who was wife to a "completely self-centered literary man," was also a writer of only "very slender talents." In publishing her stories, H. G. Wells carried out, according to Porter, a cruelty all the more effective for its subtlety.

Generally Porter was averse to radicalism in any form, and she objected to radical feminism because, she implied, it lost sight of general human oppression, a large fact of life as Porter had seen it. Even some of her strongest feminist stands are qualified with reminders that a larger picture encompasses women's plight. In "Sex and Civilization," for example, Porter said that "to indict women as slave-minded is to remind us that the human race is by nature slavish. The oppressive individual is merely a slave who has momentarily got the upper hand of his fellow bondsmen." Porter at one point even objected to the term *feminist,* as it was used to describe Genevieve Taggard, a poet and a friend of Porter's. Porter offered "modern" as an alternative to "feminist," which, she said, is quite meaningless as a term used to describe a poet ("A Singing Woman"). Taggard is "modern in the sense that she belongs to her time, and therefore does not assume female poses merely pleasing to the eye." Porter had considered herself modern for many years, probably from the time she left family and Texas behind her and went to Chicago. Her concept of the modern woman was based on certain feminist positions, but Porter was never doctrinaire, and she thought of women's liberation as a state of mind that had been just as evident in some women in the past as it was among her contemporaries. In the 1960s Porter was scornful of the vocal feminists emerging on the artistic and social scenes.[17]

Porter's final position on feminism is ambiguous only if one fails to see it in the context of her stand on other political and religious matters. Even when she was caught up in the emotions of the wars with Germany, she tempered her outrage by examining a larger human picture. In "Pale Horse, Pale Rider" she placed her contempt for patriotic propagandists beside her nightmare fear of German ravagers, and in "The Leaning Tower" she examined with detachment some of what she regarded as the causes of Germany's moral illness. Her 1945 review of Glenway Wescott's novel *Apartment in Athens* ("They Lived with the Enemy in the House") tried to lift the novel from the ranks of a diatribe. Wescott had said that his aim in the novel was to show "how bad the Germans are," but Porter, while accusing the Germans of bringing upon the world "shapeless immoderate miseries and confusions," claimed that Wescott had done something more valuable than he realized: he had "exposed and anatomized that streak of Germanism in the rest of us which made possible the Germany we know today." "Germanism," as Porter illustrated it in "The Leaning Tower" and *Ship of Fools,* grows out of intolerance and chauvinism, to which all humans, in ignorance and desperation, are inclined. This detachment often exasperated and angered those of her friends who were passionately devoted to political causes. Josephine Herbst, Porter's friend and a writer dedicated to leftist politics, believed that Porter turned away from politics and found a haven in apolitical aesthetics.[18] It was an important insight, buried in Herbst's disappointment, and it helps explain Porter's public stance on numerous issues.

Both her fiction and her nonfiction show that Porter was opposed to dogma. She was suspicious of idealism that created illusions and she despised blind obedience to any systematic way of thinking. She expressed a clear distaste for any doctrine that promoted materialism or self-interest at the expense of others' dignity. In her 1926 review of the letters of Rosalie Caden Evans ("La Conquistadora") Porter confirmed her dislike of imperialism at the same time that she identified her sympathies with the Mexican revolution. Mrs. Evans, an American, and her husband, Harry Evans, an Englishman, had lost their considerable Mexican property during the Madero revolution of 1910 and had left Mexico in anger and frustration. After her husband's death Mrs. Evans returned to Mexico to try to regain her property. She assumed squatter's rights in one of her haciendas and held off at gunpoint agents of the revolutionary government, which was attempting to repartition large landholdings among the Indians, an action that was symbolic of the spirit of the revolution. She declared that she would leave her holding only as a prisoner or dead, and, indeed, in August 1924 she was fatally shot in an ambush. Porter observed with an irony that looked ahead to "Flowering Judas," "Hacienda," and *Ship of Fools* that the aim of publishing the letters was "to present Mrs. Evans to a presumably outraged Anglo-Saxon world as a martyr to the sacred principles of private ownership of property: to fix her as a symbol of devotion to a holy cause."[19] In a 1928 review of Margery Latimer's novel *We Are Incredible* ("Misplaced Emphasis"), Porter analyzed what she called "the story of pauper spirits and confusion of values" and asked whether "this misplaced emphasis" was a symptom of "some dangerous disease eating at the vitals of young Americans." She said that it was.

Many of the world's problems seemed to Porter to be born out of intolerance for other values and ways of life. She was especially sensitive to religious intolerance, which she depicted in all its varieties in *Ship of Fools*. She gathered evidence for years. In the 1920s, while living in Salem, Massachusetts, Porter became interested in Cotton Mather and began writing a biography of him that she never finished. The three chapters she did finish and publish as separate essays show Mather to be a self-righteous and vain man who promoted anything but true religion. Porter's mind was focused on this subject when she reviewed *Cotton Mather: Keeper of the Puritan Conscience* ("The Dark Ages of New England") and in 1929 *The Devil Is a Woman*, a group of poems by Alice Mary Kimball ("Moral Waxworks Exposed"). Porter might have been speaking of her own research when she declared in the latter review, "I have been ushered through a museum of spiritual horrors, where pietist dogma is disclosed in the various shapes of meanness and noble theories of conduct have incarnated themselves stiffened into the postures of fanaticism." When Porter reviewed George F. Willison's *Saints and Strangers*, a history of the Puritans who settled in America, she described herself as "a student of the period" and concluded that the Puritans' "virtues are simply not great enough to overbalance their disturbing lack of charm. And I wish I might never have to hear again that they brought the idea of political and religious freedom to this country. It got in in spite of them, and has had rough going ever since, which is the fault of all of us." [20]

While Porter's book reviews reveal her public positions on religion, politics, and social issues, they are even more important for what they reveal about her aesthetic values. In her reviews she established her models and her standards, she defined art, and she described the responsibility of the artist as she saw it. Porter named her models—her teachers—as Laurence Sterne, [21] Virginia Woolf, Jane Austen, Emily Brontë, Henry James, W. B. Yeats, James Joyce, [22] T. S. Eliot, and Ezra Pound, [23] all writers she consistently set apart from the other good, steady artists she simply admired: Edna St. Vincent Millay ("The Poet and Her Imp"), Katherine Mansfield, Willa Cather, Edith Sitwell, Colette ("A Most Lively Genius"), and

Dylan Thomas.[24] Porter wrote generally favorable reviews of works
by Genevieve Taggard ("A Singing Woman"), Esther Forbes ("Hand-
Book of Magic"), Margery Latimer ("Misplaced Emphasis"), Josephine
Herbst ("The Family" and "Bohemian Futility"), Kay Boyle ("Example to the Young"), Caroline Gordon ("Dulce et Decorum Est"),
and François Boyer ("This Strange, Old World"). In every instance
Porter admired truthfulness, craftsmanship, imagination, independence from imitation, freedom from dogma or message, simplicity,
and grace. Porter thought that truthfulness lay beyond research and
facts. It is the truth of feeling, as Miranda says in "Old Mortality."
It is what Porter praised D. H. Lawrence for in *The Plumed Serpent,*
even when she judges the book a failure as a book about Mexico. She
was able to say that the triumph of the novel as a work of art lies in
Lawrence's gaining, "by sheer poetic power," a mystical truth that
transcends his "confusions, obsessions, and occult dogma."[25]

Porter placed much value on hard work rather than spontaneous
writing, a distinction she characterized as the difference between the
Whitman-minded writers and the James-minded writers; she was,
she said, on the side of James.[26] Porter said of Margery Latimer, "She
has worked honestly, and has not neglected to sharpen and polish
the tools of her craft. This is a mark of a good guildsman in any age"
("Misplaced Emphasis"). The failure of craftsmanship was the fault
of William Goyen's *The House of Breath,* as Porter saw it, just as
François Boyer's *The Secret Game* was "well-made" ("This Strange,
Old World").

Porter considered imagination to go hand in hand with truth-
telling as active agents for the good artist. Reviewing *The Stones
Awake: A Novel of Mexico* (1936), she accused Carleton Beals of
having insufficient imagination to write good fiction ("History on
the Wing"). Beals was a friend of Porter's, and she had used him and
his wife Lillian as models for the journalist and Miriam in her story,
"That Tree," published two years before. She praised Beals as much
as she honestly could, saying he was a first-rate journalist but not a
very good novelist: "He cannot follow his characters into the locked
doors of their hearts and minds because he did not create them."

The exception was Esperanza, an Indian village girl, no doubt created from a model, said Porter slyly, and Porter recommended the book for the mere opportunity of knowing Esperanza. (In "That Tree" the journalist lives with an Indian girl while Miriam is in retreat in the United States.)

Porter charged John Cowper Powys with both lack of imagination and artistic dishonesty in his novel *Ducdame* ("Over Adornment"). Although he produced "religion, folk superstitions, ancient legend and poetry, the pagan gods and scraps of modern psychology to aid him in breathing life into his story," and although he "describes and explains and agitates, . . . nothing breathes or stirs." Powys's men and women are "reduced to pale symbols," and the author does not have a "firm hold of the clews leading from surface irrelevancy of conduct to the forces working secretly, with power and harmony at the bottom of life." A failure of imagination, in fact, invites slavish imitation. Porter praised many of her contemporaries who "would have resented, and rightly, the notion of discipleship or of interdependence" ("Example to the Young").

Porter was particularly firm on the distinction between art and propaganda or between art and works that make a moral point. She criticized Emily Post for pursuing "an apostolic" mission, as "apologist of society," and concluded that Post's bad novel *Parade* unwittingly teaches the moral "that Literature and Etiquette make bad bed fellows" ("Etiquette in Action"). In 1926 Porter reviewed a biography of Daniel Boone written by Stewart Edward White for children ("History for Boy and Girl Scouts"). In the review she recalled that her own childhood picture of Boone was "singularly unattractive" because of the moralistic idealization of the man, a theme she had presented ironically several years earlier in "The Martyr." Porter, who called herself "a respectable admirer of children," believed that children have an honesty that cuts through to truth, as she stressed in an essay titled "Children and Art," published the following year in the *Nation*. White, she said, made Boone come alive "without the prunes of moral," only pointing a moral at the very tag end, "where any quick-witted child may spot it at a glance: and so close the book."

Messages and morals come in many forms, but none has a place in art. Porter wrote a devastating review of Polly Boyden's *The Pink Egg,* a political allegory about, in Porter's words, "downtrodden, underprivileged sparrows who make a revolution and throw all the robins and other handsomer, luckier, and more talented birds out of the orchard where they live, and some of the very nicest robins turn in and help them." While Porter questioned the sense of Boyden's choosing sparrows and of her using the lighthouse to symbolize "the danger of turning the world over to the sparrows," it is clear that Porter was more offended by the heavy-handed message. She concluded, "As for these birds with their unpleasantly human ways, I am reminded irresistibly of the beachcomber's fable about the man who tried to make the mice in his house wear little wool hats during the cold weather. He wasn't any more successful than Miss Boyden trying to make her birds wear waistcoats, but he was a great deal funnier."

Porter faced a dilemma when reviewing friends' works that did not meet her critical standards. She solved the problem by praising what she honestly could and leaving unstated her complaints. Josephine Herbst's works, for example, were usually laden with messages, offensive, regardless of the content, to Porter's concept of art. Consequently, she praised Herbst's living characters in *Nothing Is Sacred* but was content to finish the review by summarizing the plot and cryptically recommending a particular segment of the work because "it is as much above the average in narrative power as it is in the interest of the material" ("The Family"). Herbst's *Money for Love* has an even more blatant political message which Porter could not quite ignore. She argued that people like Herbst's characters do not exist in real life, but she modified the criticism by saying that Herbst, "a good artist, perfectly in command of her method," has for her own "mysterious reasons" chosen to make them live in fiction.

Porter praised Virginia Woolf highly for keeping her work free of dogma. Woolf, said Porter, "had no plan whatever for her personal salvation, or the personal salvation even of someone else, brought no doctrine: no dogma." Porter in fact described Woolf as "the artist": "She was full of secular intelligence primed with the profane virtues, with her love not only of the world of all the arts created by the human imagination, but a love of life itself and of daily living, a spirit at once gay and severe, exacting and generous, a born artist and a sober craftsman."[27]

Porter had a reverential attitude toward the artist, and she thought of true art and pure religion as serving the same purpose: giving meaning and form to "the chaos" we call life. "A Quaker Who 'Had a Splendid Time of It'" is Porter's review of *The Letters of Hannah Whitall Smith*, the mother of Logan Pearsall Smith and herself a celebrated Quaker preacher and writer of religious books. While the review conveys Porter's undisguised admiration for Hannah Smith, it is perhaps more significant for an incidental comment she made and for an anecdote she chose to cite. Smith had been impressed by two lectures by Oscar Wilde, who had said, "To the true artist there is no time but the artistic moment; and no land but the land of beauty." Hannah Smith remarked, "He does say now and then a fine thing about art, just about what I would say about religion." Porter obviously approved, for the statement confirmed her contention that art and religion have the same sources and offer the only possibilities for finding meaning in life. In her review of Marian Storm's *The Life of Saint Rose* ("The First American Saint") Porter made subtle comments about paternal authority, but she also observed that "saints create themselves as works of art." Devoted and practical churchmen "fear them and fight them, and end by absorbing and canonizing them."

If many of her reviews reveal what Porter thought about a great number of subjects, still others help explain her fictional techniques. "Ay, Que Chamaco" [What a brat] is a review of a collection of caricatures by Miguel Covarrubias, a good friend whose work Porter admired. The review is especially important for its implicit explanation of an important aspect of Porter's style. Porter saw in good caricature, "a well seasoned tradition" in Mexico, the "deadly discernment of the comic in the other person, together with each man's grave regard for his own proper dignity."[28] According to Porter, Covarrubias was the best because with only a few bold strokes he could link the outer appearance of his subject to an inner quality, perhaps one the subject has taken pains to hide. The simplicity and economy of line in caricature, and the irony and wit implicit in it, are congruent with Porter's classical style of writing, which was already developed by the 1920s. The argument is even more convincing when one learns that Porter also drew caricatures. Perhaps inspired by Covarrubias, Porter illustrated several of her reviews with line drawings, and in 1976 she provided a caricature of herself for a published collection of self-portraits of celebrities.[29]

An important element of Porter's fictional technique is her reliance on dreams or trances as devices, which she uses more frequently, and with greater point, after 1929, culminating in the three crucial dreams in "Pale Horse, Pale Rider" (1938).[30] Dreams are important also in "The Cracked Looking-Glass" (1932), "The Leaning Tower" (1941), and *Ship of Fools*. Laura's dream in "Flowering Judas" (1930) is the first use of a dream per se, as opposed to the trance of María Concepción or the deathbed reverie of Granny Weatherall. It is interesting and perhaps significant that in 1929 Porter reviewed Sylvia Townsend Warner's *The True Heart* ("The Virgin and the Unicorn"), which gave her an occasion to work out a theory about the function of dreams in fiction. Porter said of Warner's novel, "One point is interesting: the episodes and conversation are the stuff of dreams, but the inner moods of these hallucinary persons seem at times almost real. The sharp division between the actual event and the repercussion of the event on their imaginations gives the impression of a drama of reality being played in a closed house, while strangers knock noisily at the door shouting an irrelevant message." Porter said that unless she was mistaken, Warner had deliberately tried to set the reader down "in a world of symbolic truths," a phrase central to "Old Mortality."

In the same review Porter also touched upon the use of legend in fiction. Having already praised Esther Forbes for breathing out the legends she had breathed in as a child ("Hand-Book of Magic") and praising Anita Brenner, also in 1929, for the "portentous air of legend" in her book on Mexican art, Porter described Warner's theme as being "on the grand scale of legend." Porter had much to say generally about memory and legend being the proper material for the artist, and she had begun mining the legends of her childhood for stories that appeared in the 1920s, beginning with "He" and "The Jilting of Granny Weatherall," and would find their greatest expression in the Miranda cycle. Porter's abstraction of Warner's theme could, in fact, describe the theme of the Miranda stories: "Youth with its blind searching eyes walks in a waking dream of faith through adventures that would require, for a conscious mind, a desperate courage. After tremendous perils, the end is gained and the eyes are opened in amazement that so much pain had been required to gain so simple and homely a thing."

It is not possible to say with certainty that Porter took ideas from the works she reviewed. It is likely that sometimes she saw in the works of others the ideas and themes with which she had been grappling. For example, in 1928 she reviewed Esther Forbes's *Mirror for Witches* ("Hand-Book of Magic"), and at the same time she published her story "Magic," a Jamesian dialogue between a wealthy New Orleans woman and her Creole maid, who is dressing her hair. To amuse "madame," the maid tells a sordid little story about a prostitute who is obliged, through the powers of black magic, to return to the brothel she had left. The interest in Porter's story lies in its irony: black magic has not brought the prostitute back to the brothel; rather society in its complicity with evil has made it impossible for her to go anywhere else. Porter, of course, recognized that the events in Forbes's novel were brought about not by magic but by social forces. Porter said, "The true interest lies in Miss Forbes' understanding of the witch state of mind in a highly imaginative, morbidly emotional young girl." The true interest for Porter was the young girl's state of mind because she was then concerned with the subject in her own fiction, but the true center of Forbes's novel is its strong feminist statement.

Porter found other familiar themes in the books she reviewed. Her second published review, "A Self-Made Ghost" (1924), is a consideration of W. L. George's novel *The Triumph of Gallio*. According to Porter, George's hero is full of "self-love," and the whole work was really "a thesis on how to rationalize an incapacity to love." By 1932 she had written about a mother's inability to love her idiot son ("He"), a young woman's incapacity for love ("Theft"), a young woman's unwillingness to love ("Flowering Judas"), the relationship between love and hate ("Rope"), and the perversion of love ("Hacienda"). Illusion about love was a theme in two of Porter's already published stories, "The Martyr" and "Virgin Violeta," and she treated it again in "The Cracked Looking-Glass" (1932). *Ship of Fools* may even be considered a treatise on the various forms and disguises of love and hate.

Considered collectively, Porter's book reviews are reflections of her aesthetics, her worldview, and the themes and subjects that fill her fiction. Neither an academician nor a rigid thinker, Porter approached others' works with a freshness and what she might have called a poet's perspective rather than a fact gatherer's viewpoint. It is a distinction she made between science and art,[31] and it was what Malcolm Cowley had in mind when he commented about the loose paragraphs in one of her reviews but added that the people who could construct tight paragraphs also could not write as well as Porter.[32] Porter attended to book reviewing much the same way she wrote fiction: both kinds of writing were exercises of the imagination. Some of the reviews are critically slight and are most important only for Porter's personal comments, but others, such as "This Strange, Old World," and "Example to the Young," are astute critical analyses by a perceptive artist.[33]

Notes

1. See the appendix for a list of the reviews included in *The Collected Essays and Occasional Writings of Katherine Anne Porter* (New York: Delacorte Press, 1970; hereinafter referred to as *The Collected Essays*).

2. *My Chinese Marriage* (New York: Asia Publishing Company, 1922).

3. Barbara Thompson, "The Art of Fiction XXIX—Katherine Anne Porter: An Interview," *Paris Review*, no. 29 (1963): 97.

4. See "The Mexican Trinity" and "Where Presidents Have No Friends," *The Collected Essays*, 399–415.

5. *Outline of Mexican Popular Arts and Crafts* (Los Angeles: Young and McCallister, 1922).

6. "Corridos," *Survey* 52 (May 1, 1924): 157–59.

7. "The Guild Spirit in Mexican Art (as told to Katherine Anne Porter by Diego Rivera)," *Survey* 52 (May 1, 1924): 174–78. See also "From a Mexican Painter's Notebooks," *Arts* 7 (January 1925): 21–23.

8. Porter names, without additional comment, the following: *The Formative Years*, by Henry Adams; *The James Family*, by F. O. Matthiessen; and *The Making of Yesterday*, by Raoul de Roussy de Sales ("Books I Have Liked," *New York Herald Tribune Weekly Book Review*, December 7, 1947); *On the Limits of Poetry*, by Allen Tate; *The White Goddess*, by Robert Graves; and *The Moment and Other Essays*, by Virginia Woolf ("Books I Have Liked," *New York Herald Tribune Weekly Book Review*, December 5, 1948); *Nineteen Eighty-four*, by George Orwell; *The Golden Apples*, by Eudora Welty; *Willa Cather on Writing*, by Willa Cather; *The Hero with a Thousand Faces*, by Joseph Campbell; *The Journals of Andre Gide, 1928–1939*, vol. 3, trans. Justin O'Brien; *The Diaries of Franz Kafka, 1914–1923*; *A Barbarian in Asia*, by Henri Michaux; *Lorca: The Poet and His People*, by Arturo Barea; *Benjamin Constant*, by Harold Nicolson; and *The Latin Poets*, ed. Francis R. B. Godolphin ("The Best Books," *New York Times Book Review*, December 4, 1949).

9. *The Days Before* (New York: Harcourt, Brace, 1952), vii.

10. KAP to Genevieve Taggard, June 5, 1926; unpublished letter, KAP Collection, the McKeldin Library, University of Maryland.

11. Porter's references to machinery in this review, as well as in "Quetzalcoatl" (*The Collected Essays*, 421–25), prefigure the symbolism and imagery in "Flowering Judas" and "Hacienda."

12. See Jane Flanders, "Katherine Anne Porter's Feminist Criticism: Book Reviews from the 1920's," *Frontiers* 4.2 (1979): 44–48.

13. *The Collected Essays*, 187–92.

14. "Quetzalcoatl," *The Collected Essays*, 423.

15. "Dylan Thomas," *The Collected Essays*, 126.

16. "On Christopher Sykes," *The Collected Essays*, 64–67.

17. See Joan Givner, *Katherine Anne Porter: A Life* (New York: Simon and Schuster, 1982), 461.

18. See, e.g., Josephine Herbst to James Farrell, n.d., 7 Rue Cels, Paris (XIV) France; Van Pelt Library, University of Pennsylvania. Cited by Elinor Langer, *Josephine Herbst* (Boston: Atlantic/Little, Brown, and Company, 1984), 194.

19. *The Collected Essays*, 417.

20. See "Pull Dick, Pull Devil," *The Collected Essays*, 144.

21. See "The Winged Skull," *The Collected Essays*, 81–85.

22. See "Virginia Woolf," *The Collected Essays*, 68–71.

23. See "It Is Hard to Stand in the Middle," *The Collected Essays*, 40–46. In her first review of Gertrude Stein's work ("Everybody Is a Real One"), Porter was highly complimentary of Stein's talent and influence, and in the 1920s she frequently named Stein among the writers who had influenced her. Her opinion of Stein changed drastically, as is apparent in the second review ("Second Wind"), a parody of Stein's style, and in later essays and letters Porter wrote. See "Gertrude Stein: Three Views," *The Collected Essays*, 251–70.

24. See "The Art of Katherine Mansfield," *The Collected Essays*, 47–52; "Reflections on Willa Cather," *The Collected Essays*, 29; for Sitwell, see "The Laughing Heat of the Sun," *The Collected Essays*, 58–63; "Dylan Thomas," *The Collected Essays*, 123–24.

25. "Quetzalcoatl," *The Collected Essays*, 423.

26. See "Three Statements about Writing," *The Collected Essays*, 452.

27. "Virginia Woolf," *The Collected Essays*, 71.

28. In her review of Max Beerbohm's *And Even Now* ("Beerbohm Bailiwick") Porter also praised the caricatures by Beerbohm. See "Max Beerbohm," *The Collected Essays*, 75–76.

29. Porter supplied drawings for "The Great Catherine," "Quetzalcoatl," "A Singing Woman," and "Everybody Is a Real One." Her self-portrait appears in *Self-Portrait* (New York: Random House, 1976), 4.

30. See Thomas Walsh, "The Dream's Self in 'Pale Horse, Pale Rider,'" *Wascana Review* 14.2 (Fall 1979): 61–79.

31. See "On a Criticism of Thomas Hardy," *The Collected Essays*, 7.

32. Malcolm Cowley to KAP, April 9, 1941; unpublished letter, the Cowley Collection, the Newberry Library, Chicago.

33. Porter's review of Kay Boyle's works ("Example to the Young") is included in *The Critic as Artist*, ed. Gilbert A. Harrison (New York: Liveright, 1972). The essays are described as a "collection of sixty outstanding literary essays."

"This Strange, Old World" and Other Book Reviews
  by Katherine Anne Porter

✍ Mexico

New York Herald Tribune Books, November 2, 1924, p. 9.

Review of *A Gringo in Mañanaland,* by Harry L. Foster (New York: Dodd, Mead and Company, 1924); and *Beautiful Mexico,* by Vernon Quinn (New York: Frederick A. Stokes Company, 1924).

Mme. Calderon de la Barca looked at life in Mexico, about three-quarters of a century ago, with the eyes of an ardent, candid and witty mind. After her letters home were published it became rather the fashion to write about Mexico. For a heavy length of time an ominous library on the subject swelled and mouldered. Then, in the early part of this century, Charles Flandrau wrote *Vive México.* So now we have two living books rescued from the growing rubbish heap which is the literature about Mexico in the English language. And still the heap grows, and still there is no revisitation to any page in it of those qualities which gave life to these two books: poetic emotion, gayety, discrimination.

A Gringo in Mañanaland is a book as graceless as its title. The author seems habitually to do this sort of thing, judging from the list of books given under his name on the slip cover. This present work is the optical record of a touring newspaper man in Mexico and several South American states. It is smart, opinionated, observant, bursting with easy good will. The story goes rattling along full tilt like a popular stage comedy, everything happening neatly in full view of the audience. Buried cities, cathedrals, revolutions and social customs are viewed affably, with the raffish eye of one who sees every surface and misses every core. The author has a sincere, if not at all a comprehending, affection for the countries he visits. He strikes up with fresh acquaintances at every turn, and likes them all, with the slightly patronizing air of the professional globe trotter toward the person who stays at home and creates local color for the tourist. If now and then his rash acceptances are brought to pause, it is only for a moment. He finds an explanation as he flits, and brightly embraces all. Happily, he has no political message to deliver, which rather takes the curse off the whole thing.

Beautiful Mexico, by Vernon Quinn, is quite a heavy book, designed to entertain and instruct the General Public, who may not have read anything about Mexico. The main points of Mexican history have been given a careful restatement, with many less familiar details, added from documents loaned from the archives of the National Museum of Mexico, the National Library and the Public Library of Puebla. Every chapter is gravid with a full hundredweight of diverse information. Legend and history, descriptions of scenery and Indian folk customs, a few thrilling passages from Spanish pirate tales, populations and industries are set down in a heap, all very painstaking, blameless and uninspired.

The author believes the United States must eventually intervene down there, for Mexico's own shining good. Obliquely, the reason is given in the chapter following, in a résumé of the wealth of that fabulous country. There are mines of gold and silver, mountains of iron and opals, seas of pearls and rivers of oil, fattened cattle and forests of fine woods. It reminds one of Prester John's letter to the King of France. . . . Even the butterflies are more gorgeous in Mexico than elsewhere, it seems, and are being developed into a thriving industry for export.

It is very discouraging. I had hoped they might overlook the butterflies.

✍ A Self-Made Ghost

New York Herald Tribune Books, November 23, 1924, p. 3.

Review of *The Triumph of Gallio,* by W. L. George (New York: Harper and Brothers, 1924).

Mr. W. L. George has a hard, stripped metallic style, which gives curiously an effect of loquaciousness. He seems to have a fondness for characters to match, sharp-edged folk who cut both ways at once, and survive victoriously by reason of sheer toughness. In his latest work, *The Triumph of Gallio*, Mr. George, by a prudent foreword, disclaims all intellectual or social relations with Holyoake Tarrant, thereby forestalling hints of fictionized biography. This is simple desertion, for seldom has a character in fiction stood in greater need of solid sympathy and defense from his creator than Tarrant; but Mr. George distributes the responsibility among Schopenhauer, Zeno, Berkeley, and I suspect, though his name is not mentioned, Ouspensky: but most of the burden lies upon Gallio, the Roman governor; and I should like to witness his encounter in the Infinite with this, his latest disciple.

The Triumph of Gallio is the narrative of a person who steps from his cradle equipped with a tough skin, a hard heart and a blunt retentive mind. Being poor, he desires riches. He early decides that the battle is to the strong, the ruthless. If one cannot always be strong, in the intervals between strength and strength one must be sly. He starts in business as a pushcart peddler, that seeming the quickest road to freedom, and cheats housewives out of pennies. He rises in life, and sells surplus ship supplies furnished by discreet pursers. With borrowed money he buys a ship of his own, and puts aside the woman who loves him, and whom he professes to love, in order to marry a rich wife. At last he lifts the finer points of his gradually accumulating philosophy of life from a vagabond friend, and thereafter, quite seriously considers himself a self-made man.

If to be self-made is to turn every circumstance of one's life to one's own interest, he brilliantly earns the title. He gathers love here, and marriage and parenthood and wealth yonder; every one who touches his life contributes some element useful to him. Even Fate goes out of her way to assist him by killing his three children early, and causing his wife to elope with a young lover, thus proving the friability of mortal ties.

He begins to see the light: having never loved, it's no good pretending about love any longer. Having possessed enormous wealth, he loses it, and being middle aged and wearied, he decides not to make any more money. Having at last discovered, through the mind of his tramp friend, that good and evil are non-existent in a spaceless and timeless universe, that in the Infinite there are no emotions, only relationships, and that life is only the infinite minus one, he experiences a mystic and holy rapture. He fancies he has safely passed through that metaphysical process whereby one arrives at a given point and finds it identical with the point one has just quitted, the beginning and the end being one; this revelation mysteriously frees him from all things but his self-love, which was all that he had ever really possessed. On the upsurge of this conversion, he fills the family baby perambulator with odds and ends from his dismantled household, fit to sell at a penny each, and takes to the road again as a peddler. Which may or may not prove that the grafting of an intellectual metaphysical conception on a purely materialistic mind always results in meaningless activity. The true hermit, the stoic, the mystic, are silent. Tarrant is to the last a babbler, a lecturer, an explainer. He is bent on escape with a whole skin, and he covers his flight with tremendous, borrowed words.

When Paula, who loves him, attempts to follow him, she tires and must fall back, an inert gray shadow, murmuring her set phrases, making the stylized, foreordained gesture of the faithful heroine. Still talking about himself, Tarrant leaves her, and disappears into his world of invented metaphysical marvels, a grandiloquent self-made ghost trundling a perambulator full of toys to sell to other ghosts.

It is a pity Mr. George has mixed the elements of a hardy philosophy with the tag-ends of debased popular mysticism, hung it all upon Holyoake Tarrant, and called it a novel. It is really a thesis on how to rationalize an incapacity to love.

✍ The Poet and Her Imp

New York Herald Tribune Books, December 28, 1924, p. 3.

Review of *Distressing Dialogues,* by Nancy Boyd [Edna St. Vincent Millay]
(New York: Harper and Brothers, 1924).

A female child whom I greatly admire once explained to me her preference for a certain little boy. "I like him because he's such an awful
little boy. He never cares what he does or who sees him do it."

I regret being unable to place Nancy Boyd's *Distressing Dialogues*
in the hands of this infant. If I should, her mother would certainly
never speak to me again, and would snatch the companionship of
her offspring from me. For Nancy Boyd doesn't care what she says or
who hears her say it, and there is still prevalent among certain parents a tribal superstition regarding the innocence of their personal
young. So the unlucky youngest generation must wait. Later on they
will be pawing about in second-hand book shops for Millay items, as
the dealers delightfully insist on calling their odds and ends of treasure, and will find this book, on the shelf marked "Curious" and will
read in profound astonishment, wondering what the poor old souls
of 1924 could have found amusing in it.

Yet I confess I love the book. There's not a kind line in it; it is
full of low topical humor, delivered with the good middle-American
custard-pie-in-the-eye-and-a-kick-in-the-stomach technique as practiced with such drastic intelligence by Mr. Charles Chaplin before
he became high art and the subject of theses by Mr. Gilbert Seldes.

It is not generally known, perhaps (I address this review to the far-
flung reading public, and not to the 40,000 personal and dear friends
of Miss Edna St. Vincent Millay), that Nancy Boyd is more than mere
friend to the poet who has put aside the scruples of a lifetime to write
a preface to this book. Theologians would even insist that they are,
or should be, mortal enemies. . . . Let us have the truth for once:
Nancy Boyd is Edna St. Vincent Millay's lower nature.

She is the left hand of the poet which flings a brick while the right is setting down a sonnet. She is the guardian demon of the muse, the business manager who could (and did!) dig bread and butter in however modest slices out of *Vanity Fair* while the poet was writing those songs which shall give a name and a date in the future to our present American period of poetry.

It is a very Siamese twins of a literary partnership. Indeed, the famous twins seems as hostile strangers compared to the entanglement which exists between the poet and her imp. The poet sings like a throstle in a willow tree, while the imp scouts about thumbing her nose and shouting provocative obscenities in the voice of youth itself, at all things held sacred by decree of heaven.

This imp was born to fresh air, and didn't seem to be getting much at the time she wrote this book. She elbows her way through huddles of people taking tea and gin in rooms too thick with tobacco smoke. She listens to second-hand philosophy expounded by students of life who refuse to believe that their hearers might have read the same books. She watches the awful mating mechanisms of the smart middle classes, she hears hundreds of far-too-clever people being far too clever at all hours. It is all extremely amusing: so amusing that she finally gives a yell of fury and writes down: "Bride kicks maid of honor in the stomach." . . . "She stifles screams" . . . "That's mine, and if you lay one spatulate finger on it, I'll cut your heart out." It is the nervous violence of cowboys living out a winter of blizzards in too close quarters; of travelers in a small boat on a voyage too long; the exasperation of a theatrical troupe stranded in Lafayette, Louisiana, on Christmas Day. It is both symptom and result of that tautness of American nerves which D. H. Lawrence complained of when he described himself as feeling like a drawn chicken in our atmosphere. Those among us who are intellectually converted to the dogma of restraint, who crawl in our caves to do our cursing when the show gets too hot for us, should elect Nancy Boyd to be our spokesman. She is utterly unconvinced of the value of restraint as a nerve tonic. As for dogma, she shoots it on sight.

I enjoyed the *Distressing Dialogues* (so-called, probably, because two-thirds of them are not dialogues at all: this book is bent on being a joke from cover to cover) when they appeared in *Vanity Fair*. They are still amusing when gathered together in the horrid formality of an exceptionally devout binding. But I miss in this group two of the most delightful ones. The adventures of an American girl in Montparnasse, for one, and I would willingly have spared almost any chapter except, perhaps, the Impolite Letter Writer, to make space for the gorgeous fable of Diogenes and the strange woman who moved in on him and tidied up his barrel and messed up his philosophy by pointing out that he really did not need to light his lantern in the daytime.

But all this will come, no doubt, in a deep sea format supported by a God-speed-thee preface. We wait.

✍ Maya Treasure

New York Herald Tribune Books, February 9, 1925, p. 9.

Review of *In an Unknown Land*, by Thomas Gann
(New York: Charles Scribner's Sons, 1924).

This is the story of three men who boarded a boat called the *Lillian Y* (a wallowing, unloved and unlovely tub, says the chronicler) and sailed away to seek for buried treasure which lies inland from the east coast of Yucatan—a treasure cut into the piled stones which were once the temples and palaces of the lost Maya race, the founders of aboriginal American civilization. The adventurers are Dr. Gann, British archaeologist and member of the Maya Society; Dr. Sylvanus G. Morley, American archaeologist, and John Held Jr., artist.

They carried the classic paraphernalia of treasure seekers—an out-at-elbows crew, an unpardonably bad cook, a singing negro helmsman, a supply of hardtack and the special weapons of their piracy, consisting mostly of cameras, sketchbooks, measuring devices and tools for clearing pathways. They encountered storms, ran aground on sandbars, did a vast amount of wading through shark-infested shallows, hewed their way through the tough bush of strange, possibly hostile territory. And they brought back the treasure. This is, in effect, the key to the Maya system of chronology, which they discovered in the city of Tuluum. Because of this find, the work of rediscovering ancient America will be much simplified.

Dr. Gann kept a diary of the expedition. We know what songs the negro sang, what food they enjoyed—or survived—what technique of charming was employed by Held in his flirtations with the notably handsome and spirited Maya girls, what diplomacy was exercised by Dr. Morley in the frequent crises arising between the Indians and the visitors. It seems that the weather was mostly abominable, and everybody suffered alike from the malice of these abandoned peoples and from the insects, reptiles and vegetation, all equipped with stings, fangs, claws, spikes and poisonous juices. The miseries of alkali thirst, sun headache and aching feet, rain-soaked nights and sun-blistered days murmur along like a wistful obbligato to the bolder strains of derring-do. It seems harder work to find a buried city than to build a new one.

Mixed with the record of discovery are stories of the surviving forlorn fragment of Maya Indians, whose dress, food, social customs and religious ceremonies are dwindled to mere bare habit, necessity and superstitions without significance. Their religious feasts still take the form of burnt offerings, on altars shared by Maya gods and Aztec with Roman Catholic saints. Witchcraft is practiced among them, feared and profoundly believed in. The method of legal executions is unchanged from old times, the offender being chopped to pieces with a machete, the tribal weapon, a sort of primitive broadax with a short handle. Yet they have gayety and courtesy and an unyielding independence of spirit. Theoretically a part of Mexico, actually enslaved by poverty and the overpowering presence of the conqueror, they remain intractable, and only within the last four years have they consented to partially friendly relations with the Mexican government.

The scientific conclusions drawn in this book are Dr. Gann's own, with acknowledgements to Dr. Morley. The author accepts Dr. Morley's division of the Maya chronology into two main periods, embracing almost five thousand years ending about 1537, which he calls the Old Empire and the New Empire. The earliest date yet discovered, 100 B.C., is carved on a small nephrite statue found outside the Maya territory but identified as belonging to that culture. The earliest date found in a Maya city exists in Tuluum, and marks the dedication of a temple on August 28, 619 A.D.

Dr. Gann attempts no account of the origin of the Maya race. He makes no comparisons between the Maya and other parallel civilizations such as are so tempting to the explorer and the last resort of the lay enthusiast. He considers the cities as they are, and reconstructs records of the Old Empire from hieroglyphic inscriptions still standing in the ruins. For the history of the New Empire he depends on native chronicles, from which he has drawn material covering the first fifteen centuries dating from the Christian era.

The Old Empire, according to Dr. Gann, reached its apex and crumbled during the first six centuries of the Christian era, after four thousand years of life. The New Empire, a slow evolution from the old, flourished from the sixth century and endured until the Spanish conquest.

We have here the strange history of a migratory people who possessed an accurate time sense, recorded in the most perfect calendar known to the world. They were superb astronomers and mathematicians, with a complicated and eloquent system of hieroglyphic writing. Their religious expression was a beautiful and aesthetic form of nature worship until the savage Aztecs introduced the bloody Mexican rites among them, in their later times.

They created a subtle, hieratic art, working massively in stone without the aid of metals; and their wall murals, painted on iron-hard plaster, are still discernible after centuries of exposure to the destructive climate. Laboriously they upraised huge cities of stone: and mysteriously they deserted them, leaving their monuments to be devoured by the tropical jungle growths.

Dr. Gann's theory is that these migrations took place at the command of their priests and oracles, for no race was ever more bound by religious observance than the Maya, while Dr. Morley suggests that they may have been compelled by famine to seek other territory—

famine caused by gradual impoverishment of the soil under the Maya system of cultivation. Whatever the causes, the race cankered at the seed, and its greatness was declining even before the invasions of the Aztec and the Spaniard.

Divided into petty kingdoms, city fought against city under the leadership of ambitious rulers. Isolation, internecine war, weakening migrations, all contributed to the death of an agricultural race in an overpopulated country. They failed in mechanical inventiveness which leads to an industrial development, they had no agricultural implements of metal, and there seems to have been no intertribal commerce. Art, architecture and religion were their racial expressions.

In 1201 A.D. the ruler of Maya-pan went to war with the ruler of Chichen-Itza, and conquered with the help of Aztec-Toltec mercenaries, who opened the way for the Aztec influence. They brought their culture-hero-god, Quetzalcoatl, who had, by their tradition, once been a wise and benevolent living man. Now elevated to godhead, he became the Feathered Serpent. Translating his name into Cuculcan, the Maya accepted him. The Aztecs introduced their game of handball, called "tlachtli," and the Maya accepted that, gambling away their very cloaks on the wide courts of this difficult sport. The Aztecs brought also their god Chacmool, sometimes called the Tiger-god, who was until recently believed to be the Maya Bacchus, an indigenous Maya Deity, and they brought the custom of human sacrifice to the gods. . . . The Maya culture was destroyed.

Photographs, pencil maps, copies of hieroglyphics and sketches by Held are scattered plentifully throughout the text, which is written with amiable informality. Here and there Dr. Gann's purpose of writing a popular book is overcome by sheer love of science, and he lapses into technical details which will appear as so much Greek to one not familiar with the subject. But if one cares to take a little time to learn the names of the Maya months and days and the chronological terms the interest will be much increased.

Within the next few years a considerable literature may be expected on this subject, for the Carnegie Institution, under agreement with the Department of Anthropology of the Mexican government, has begun a ten-year excavation on the site of Chichen-Itza, with Dr. Morley in charge of the work. *In an Unknown Land* is, therefore, a valuable pioneer work of reference to the amateur, a textbook of suggestions for further reading.

✍ Shooting the Chutes

New York Herald Tribune Books, March 8, 1925, p. 10.

Review of *Round the World,* by Frank Hedges Butler (New York: Frederick A. Stokes Company, 1924); *Outlines of Travel,* by Harman Black (New York: Real Book Company, 1924); and *My Trip Around the World,* by Dorothy Dix (Philadelphia: Penn Publishing Company, 1924).

Now that noisy mechanical contrivances for locomotion have re-duced the earth to a vast Coney Island, traveling is no more the major adventure of heroes. Increasing numbers of individuals are getting the habit of taking a spin around the globe. Merrily they shoot the chutes in this newly opened amusement park, and gayly they come home, fresh and rosy with adventure, and write books about it. The style in travel book writing is now fixed, almost canonical—being rather more explicit than a diary, rather less entertaining than a letter home; inflated to the bursting point, because a travel book should be fat to be impressive; illustrated with a curious collection of purchased stock photographs of scenery, a few intimate camera snapshots by a member of the party and a drawing or two if the author is lucky enough to get hold of them.

We have here three such travel books by three such travelers—two professional globe trotters and one amateur. The amateur is our own Miss Dorothy Dix, and she has written much the most sponta-neous and cheerful book of the three. Technically speaking, they all went round the world. But they hit only the high spots, so that even the most determined home stayer looks in vain for mention of those loved far-off places made familiar by that prince of travel writers, Mr. Rand-McNally.

Alike familiar to Miss Dix, Mr. Harman Black and Mr. Frank

Hedges Butler are the sacred red lacquer bridge at Nikko, the Taj Ma-
hal, the Green Buddha, the bathing ghats and the burning ghats of
India, the two-fingered poi and the three-fingered poi and the dancing
girls of Hawaii. All saw, smelt and recoiled from antique eggs pickled
in lime offered them by the hospitable Chinese. The customs of foot
binding and of widow burning inspire them with an identical horror; their voices raised as one voice, they commend the scenery and
the architecture, deplore the morals and customs and describe with
nicely balanced praise and blame the food of the invaded nations.

Can it be that folk who write travel books never read any save their
own? It is, it has been, my life-long hope to travel, and, of course I
mean to write a travel book. But what shall be left to mention when
that happy day arrives? After my recent liberal—though accidental—
education in travel literature, I should hesitate to call attention to
the red lacquered bridge or the Green Buddha, though they smote
me blind with amazement. Never may I describe the burning ghats
and the bathing ghats of India now, though I might have done it so
nicely. Never may I comment on the dog-eating Coreans or a Geisha
of Nippon. And if a Sultan should give a feast with dancing girls in
my honor I should remember bitterly that he had given similar feasts
to nine hundred previous touring guests within the year just past,
and they had all gone home and put it down in books. The thought
should silence me forever.

Would I also, an Anglo-Saxon reared under the comfortable provi-
sions of American democracy, wax imperialistic in my views as my
native shores disappeared and I found myself among peoples of a sus-
piciously foreign cast of feature and habit? For our three travelers,
representing America and Great Britain, agree that India, left to her
own devices, would promptly return to her ancient darkness and the
habits of savagery which found its expression in the odd-looking,
though beautiful, temples which now attract tourists. Coreans, who
wear such screamingly funny clothes no one could possibly take
them seriously, are much better off with a Japanese clog set firmly on
the national neck. Besides, we have already noted that they relish dog
meat. Miss Dix yields to a momentary weakness. She feels sorry for

the Javanese, in a way, but only because she, personally, should hate to be colonized by the Germans or the Dutch. Otherwise, it is much more tidy for the strong nations to take care of the weak nations, and tidiness is what we need. Look at the Filipino. A most slovenly, un-Christian creature until the United States took hold of him.

Mr. Black and Mr. Hedges, being seasoned tourists, take the world's wonders much more calmly than does Miss Dix. How she did enjoy herself! How heartily she ate of the exotic delicious foods, noting that one sightsees more amiably on a full stomach! How she did squander her substance on rarities, with what light-hearted zest she trundled out to see all the classic monuments, with what gusto she fills her eyes with local color, how she does enjoy watching the antics of the natives! One photograph of Miss Dix and her party sums it all up better than a page of description. Five genteel, alert ladies, safely arrived at the age of indiscretion, are here shown wearing cork helmets, mounted on an elephant. Nestled into the howdah, they look for all the world like a brood of mythical birds, cheerful but calm, bless them, prepared for anything—almost.

The pattern varies slightly in spots. Mr. Hedges, being British, included us. He drove through the streets of New York in a Rolls-Royce car, and, in spite of his determination to see only the best of us, he cannot but note that our buildings are unnecessarily tall, and, what with prohibition and all, the United States is by no means so liberty-lighted a place as England. None the less, our Irish traffic policemen are efficient, and the patent serving doors in a certain New York hotel are convenient. He visited Old Mexico, getting as far as Tia Juana, and publishes as a souvenir a snapshot of several Nordic ladies and gentlemen looking extremely festive in sombreros and serapes furnished by the photographer. For the rest of his travels, I cannot see how he managed to avoid Miss Dix or Mr. Black.

Mr. Black's *Outlines of Travel* begins with a close-packed description of the City of London. For brevity and variety I submit that this paragraph cannot be equaled:

"In Cheapside the wife of the Duke of Gloucester walked with a white sheet over her head and holding a taper as a penance for the crime of witchcraft. In St. Alban's Church there is an hourglass over the pulpit to keep the sermons short, and in Milk Street in the same district Sir Thomas More was born."

He maintains this pace throughout.

✍ With the Enthusiasm of a Boy Scout

New York Herald Tribune Books, April 12, 1925, p. 10.

Review of *Adventures in Peru,* by Cecil H. Prodgers
(New York: E. P. Dutton, 1924).

Colonel Prodgers began his *Adventures in Peru* with what appears to be the fag end of an episode left over from his preceding book: "At the time when poor Kemmis went broke, and there was nothing doing Las Rosas way, it behooved me to look around for another job."

Who poor Kemmis was, or why he went broke, we do not learn in this volume. But Colonel Prodgers got a job superintending the breaking up of a ship stranded on the Island of Juan Fernando. The handiest, busiest person in South America he must have been; he was always getting jobs, and each new project seemed adventurous to him, so that this book is a literal record of odd chores undertaken with the enthusiasm of a Boy Scout going on his first hike. The narrative begins in Chile, dashes into Peru and hustles back and forth over South America for a space of twenty years, minus chronology, geography, plot, style, minus even material in the larger sense; yet, sustained by nothing more tangible than the fervent desire to tell, the pilgrim has managed a book which has the value of a literary curio and has given an unconscious self-portrait which a more sophisticated man would have taken pains to touch up.

He had the habit of starting long, involved stories, as, for example, how he happened to meet a certain interesting woman. But he got sidetracked describing a stolen dog, presumably hers, and the scheme by which he outwitted the thief. Somehow the story never got told, for the dog reminded him of something else, and off he bounded, finishing up a thousand miles away and ten years later, in the middle of another situation.

South America charmed him completely, and in his bluff British gentry style he got along famously with everybody and had a great time doing his jobs and getting his bits of money. He combined ship-wrecking with a small dried fish business and horse training with mine prospecting, and in his spare hours he hunted and fished and got acquainted with the Indians. Once he cured a man of his rheumatism, though he cannily refuses to reveal the process to us, and in gratitude the man told the exact location of a fabulous treasure buried in French Bay. No sooner was he all prepared to go treasure hunting than some one offered him a steady job training racehorses, and he took that instead.

Shrewd and childish, gullible and calculating, it never occurred to him to doubt the evidence of his senses, and they played some antic games on him. He was a luminous believer in signs and wonders and Peruvian sovereign remedies. He heard and saw strange things that could, in retrospect, pass for ghosts. And on two occasions, while voyaging off the Island of Fernando de Noronha, on nothing more befogging than a little beer and several beef sandwiches, he saw a sea serpent.

He was in a state of perpetual excitement over the present, and tomorrow promised to be even more entertaining. To him everything was worth mentioning merely because it happened, and so we find a bookfull of strange items, naïve confidences, marvelous schemes for making money, a minute account of trades involving a pound or two, the names and records of horses he had trained, scraps of conversation about nothing in particular with people of whom the reader never heard and will never hear again; it all hasn't the slightest importance, yet I certainly read it straight through, and it delighted me. . . . *The Young Visitors* delighted me in its time.

✍ Over Adornment

New York Herald Tribune Books, July 5, 1925, p. 12.

Review of *Ducdame*, by John Cowper Powys (Garden City, N.Y.: Doubleday, Page and Company, 1925).

A Greek invocation derived at third hand from Shakespeare may serve to call fools into a circle. A dedication to Kwang-Tze of Khiyuan, that Superior Man, testifies to the personal philosophical tastes of the author. But a living book cannot be made from fragments ransacked from literature and pieced together by an effort of the will.

From a great store of reference and recollection Mr. Powys has produced religion, folk superstitions, ancient legend and poetry, the pagan gods and scraps of modern psychology to aid him in breathing life into his story and into his people. He describes and explains and agitates, but nothing breathes or stirs, not even the leaves nor the talkative, aimless lips of the women. The story remains untold, disguised and corrupted with words, and the men and the women are reduced to pale symbols, interpreted by a conventionalized psychoanalysis which cannot free itself from romantic mysticism. Their quite accountable words and deeds are clothed with a solemn profundity, they are dissected with a bookish preoccupation for the problems of feeling; they think their simple smooth-worn thoughts in heavy book English, which weighs them down and robs them of life.

They are not created or even invented; they are merely contrived from a set of things remembered through a fog of preconceptions and a will to grandeur. Human monsters, shapes of sin, haunt the story in the form of two bastard children of old Squire Ashover. A half-wit, Binnorie, a creature timeless and wild, roams about on grotesque, inhuman mischief. Of the two brothers Lexie is an invalid satyr and Rook a sort of negative Don Juan, and neither of them has either energy or imagination enough for love, yet women love them hopelessly. Even their love of nature is ritualistic, and they delight to people the woods with ghosts and figures of legend. They cannot even love a tree for its own sake, but must clothe it down with mystic veil upon mystic veil until the divinely simple form is spoiled.

Lady Ann's knee is never beautiful in its proper substance and contour. It is merely "a knee that might have belonged to Artemis herself." And her mouth is a perfect Cupid's bow.

The bells ring in the chapel at Ashover and a man listens to them. He has lived there all his life, and his ancestors lived and died there for centuries, within sound of them, and he loves them with intimate association. Yet "it is as if the gigantic feet of Cybele herself, Magna Mater, Bona Dea, were striding bronze sandaled," . . . etc., etc. Aside from the mere confusion of coupling the Greek-named goddess with her attributes in the Latin, why should not the imagination of the listener have been touched by those ringing bells with something more fresh and true than a tattered phrase from the schoolbook psychology?

Nell, the parson's wife, encounters a hurrying crisis in her love for Rook Ashover. She pauses, sentimentally as a heroine in any lady's book, to bury her face in a vase of pale virginal blooms, and there ensues a paragraph of shockingly bad writing, involving two quotations, to describe rotundly what might have been told so simply—that for a moment she was free of the torments of jealousy.

The scene in which Lady Ann and Nell, bitterly jealous of each other, sing in strophe and antistrophe the courtier's song from *As You Like It* (the song and its source being set down carefully) is absurd and painful; jealous women, even symbolic ones, are rarely so picturesque, and if they are they should go on the stage at once and not waste their talents in an English countryside.

When the parson, running to murder Rook on the Foulden Bridge, comes upon his victim, the author stops to point out that it "might easily have seemed like one single man encountering his own image, or even meeting a phantom of himself, as Goethe once did on an unfrequented road; but no such fancy as that crossed the mind of William Hastings." But unfortunately it crossed the literary memory of the author, and for some dark reason he is impelled to point out the curious fact that William Hastings differed strangely from Goethe.

But for once we see a character conducting himself almost indepen-
dently of his inventor, hastening to his unhappy destiny honestly
cleansed of classic comparisons.

Lady Ann, seeing the full moon, is instantly reminded of "Astarte,
queen of the heavens, with crescent horns." And Lexie, after many
hesitations, finally seduces Nell, taking refuge from the rain in a pile
of hay in an open barn, which becomes by obvious association, a
shrine of Demeter.

These things are endless; meant to adorn the idea, they have
smothered it. The whole story is founded on secret and personal
things, almost too secret and personal to have been only half revealed,
since now they are neither mysterious nor clear, only hopelessly confused. Nowhere are we made to feel that the author has got firm
hold of the clews leading from surface irrelevancy of conduct to the
forces working secretly, with power and harmony, at the bottom of
life. Unless the mind of the seeker is clear, these forces cast up signs
altogether divided and misleading. Mr. Powys has taken upon himself the burden of interpreting petty complexities in terms of high
tragedy, and the effect is similar to that produced by bad actors in a
great play, badly learned, in no wise comprehended.

✍ Sex and Civilization

New York Herald Tribune Books, July 5, 1925, pp. 3–4.

Review of *Our Changing Morality, A Symposium,* ed. Freda Kirchwey
(New York: Albert and Charles Boni, 1924).

Originally published as a series by the *Nation,* these essays are now
presented as a unit, edited and prefaced by Freda Kirchwey. A group of
men and women gathered in a round table discussion, being reasonable about sex, is always an edifying spectacle, and a comparatively
modern one. Heretofore such gatherings have furnished the excuse
for much wit, much bantering, much merry double entendre; the
atmosphere has always been more personal than scientific.

This is a calm book, and very few of the contributors have found the subject diverting. Fearlessly, keeping cool heads and careful vocabularies, they have examined this combustible subject, its unhappy past, its disreputable present, its gloomy future. Law, philosophy, literature, science and sociology are represented here, and each member states clearly that, from whatsoever point of view, sex is a serious problem. Not one of them is bold enough to suggest a drastic solution that will be perceptible to this generation, or even the next. They agree that it needs more time, more intelligence and understanding, sounder heads and gentler hearts.

Several of the collaborators profess to have no hopes in the matter, yet they suggest changes, hopefully, changes in human nature as we have learned it; others lay down tentative private rules not entirely applicable to mankind as a whole; still others think the state of affairs is no better, and is rapidly growing worse. They agree, nevertheless, that morality is changing visibly in our day.

Bertrand Russell opens the discussion with "Styles in Ethics." He applies the cooling touch at once, lifting sex out of the realm of frenzy and viewing it as an element of life to be controlled on a basis of ethical behavior, an inner freedom regulated by the individual with a right regard for his personal responsibilities. Romanticists, who notoriously muddle their private lives, have much to learn from Mr. Russell, but I doubt if romanticists read him. If human beings were born ethical and intelligent, or even if a modest number of them could be trained up that way, Mr. Russell's conclusions would be applicable. As it is, he reasons it out and washes his hands: "It is the business of the mystic, the artist, the poet," he says. This brings us to Edwin Muir, a most fastidiously resolved compound of the three.

"Women—Free for What?" inquires Mr. Muir, gloomily. His answer is discouraging. Woman is no more free than a democracy is free: both have a slave's idea of freedom. They do not ask for equal joys, but for equal obligations, the mere liberty to serve and work. He concludes that we are all bound to a mechanical, leisureless, joyless conception of duty and labor. Men and women alike can find refuge only in a "deliberate and reasonable light heartedness."

With precisely this kind of light heartedness, Miss Isabel Leavenworth, a philosopher in good standing, asks boldly and clearly for equal joys, such as they are. These are not only the joys of art, of social and legal recognition, of intellectual liberty, but the joys of love. She calls her essay "Virtue for Women," and makes it plain that this virtue places too much value on a state of physical intactness and far too little on moral quality. Moreover, "virtue" is a shameful article of merchandise, bought by one woman in a hard bargain with another woman; it does the one of them not much credit, and the other too much dishonor. And in the end neither benefits thereby.

Charlotte Perkins Gilman belongs to a generation which clicks the tongue and lifts the eyebrow at the connection, even in the words, of "joy" and "sex." She stems in turn from a generation of women which labored more hopelessly under the disabilities of sex than any since the fifteenth century. The savor of that bitterness is still in her speech; she utters the old womanly resentment against two-sided morality, with the seamy side turned toward women. She still regards woman as a creature over-specialized in sex, victim of the ranging greedy passions of men. In this present day, seeing what we see of the activities of women in love, this view of woman as victim and instrument is almost incomprehensible. It offends the sex pride of latter day women, an ancient pride which once took the inverted form of slave-mindedness, it is true, but to indict women as slave-minded is to remind us that the human race is by nature slavish. The oppressive individual is merely a slave who has momentarily got the upper hand of his fellow bondsmen. Mrs. Gilman is profoundly disturbed by the growing laxity of the marriage tie and the increasing casual attitude toward love—two things noted as signs of health by another observer. Monogamy is her cure. "Now, this view of love is not new," says Edwin Muir. "It has always been dear to the bourgeoisie, who thought it a matter of immense moment that they should have sons to carry on their businesses when they were dead." It was dear to the feminists of the last century, too, who could not, or would not, accept sexual freedom for themselves, and therefore would have forbidden it to their men. But the men know better, as Miss Leavenworth has pointed out.

"Where Are the Women Geniuses?" inquires Sylvia Kopald in advancing the theory that on the freedom enjoyed by men depends the breadth of their achievements in the arts. Once woman gains this freedom, a mental state springing from a sense of liberation from the petty personal demands of others, she will also do great work in the arts. "Not so," rejoins Alexander Goldenweiser, in effect, discussing "Men and Women as Creators." Firmly he points out that woman's greatest work of art is the child and that her creativeness expresses itself best in domestic craftsmanship. This is as it should be, he believes, and is in nowise disposed to quarrel with things as they are. No one liberates the male genius save himself, says Mr. Goldenweiser, and his conclusion is that this capacity for self-liberation is a male characteristic.

Beatrice M. Hinkle, in "Women and the New Morality," adds weight to this assertion by her admission, which is also an accusation: "Woman was made a symbol or personification of man's morality. She had to live for him what he was unable to live for himself. That was the reason for his indignation at moral transgressions on her part. She had injured the symbol and revealed his weakness to him." This leads me to believe there may be some truth in what Mr. Goldenweiser says, granting first the truth of Miss Hinkle's statement. He assigns women to first rank in the art of acting, which is two-thirds interpreting and one-third dissembling. The actress is a plastic medium for the expression of some one else's idea. She is creative only in so far as she can conceive this idea, add to it her own essential quality and bring forth from the thought germ a full born interpretation. Why did woman allow herself to be used as a symbol by man? If this difference is biological, then it may be said that nature is the implacable enemy of woman, and it is the duty of intelligence to combat this destructive law. Nature can be conquered by persuasion, by patience. It is a long process of tree grafting, of seed mixing.

In "Love and Marriage" Ludwig Lewisohn believes that men and women are becoming gradually accustomed to the fact, long denied or disguised, that they cannot love each other except by occasional fits, and those not for long. "Love in itself is rare, and married love is perhaps as rare as beauty or genius," he ends.

But what about friendship? "Can men and women be friends?" asks

Floyd Dell, plaintively. His answer seems to be that some can and some can't. Social customs forbid, wives and husbands grow jealous, sex itself is almost bound to intervene. The path of mixed friendship is perilous, therefore delicious and exciting. Possible only if the head is level enough. Problem: Find the level head.

M. Vaerting contributes a clever essay on "Dominant Sexes," making a semi-scientific effort to prove that Nature is fairer than we think, and pursues a turn-and-turn-about policy, giving the leadership first to one sex and then the other, in rhythmic cycles. "The subordinate sex," says he, "whether male or female, seeks ornament," and points to the past as evidence that, at various stages of our human development, the balance of power has shifted alternately between men and women, with a corresponding shift of dress and decoration from the dominant sex to the subordinate. It is an entertaining thesis, somewhat bound out by the sartorial habits of the animal kingdom, where the unadorned female rules in the mating season, taking her own time, knowing well that when she is ready for a mate she can have her choice of the most beautifully arrayed and virile among the males. Yet, humanly considered, there are a few gaps in the theory which badly want filling before the ladies can take much comfort of it.

Other reasonable analyses of the gradual change which goes on always in the relations of men and women, with special reference to recent surface change, are contained in essays by Arthur Garfield Hays, Elsie Clews Parsons, Joseph Wood Krutch, Florence Guy Seabury and Louis Fischer. It is entertaining to note that even among these minds there is a perceptible pull-and-haul between the male and the female viewpoint. The women are more minute, realistic, explicit and urgent. They have been feeding babies by the hour glass for millions of years, and they know that to be effective, practical things must be done immediately. The men are largely content to advance by cycles of evolution. It is the difference in gait between the shod and the free foot. But one or two of the women have unshod themselves, and there is a notable gayety in their newly taken stride.

The mere fact of such a collaboration getting itself written and published is a good sign of improving health in the social life among civilized men and women. Their conclusions here are based on thought, not feeling. In general, men and women prefer not to think about love, and sex will probably remain, much as it has been, on a plane of instinct rather sadly corrupted by civilization. For sex is not inimical to life, but only to organized society, which appears, in retrospect and from a female point of view, to have been a unified expression of hatred and protest against life itself.

✍ The Complete Letter Writer

New Republic, vol. 44, no. 562 (September 9, 1925), pp. 77–78.

Review of *Original Letters from India (1779–1815)*, by Eliza Fay
(New York: Harcourt, Brace and Company, 1925).

In his foreword to these letters, Mr. Forster states that Mrs. Fay is a work of art, and adds that she was also a historical character. It is true she is a work of art, and as such has received full critical appreciation from Mr. Forster in two acute studies, recently published, entitled "Eliza in Chains," and "Eliza in Egypt." If her own documents are less entertaining, yet they are needed in order to give reality to this lady, and persuade the reader that Mr. Forster did not create her, in a gently malicious mood, for his own amusement. He has taken pains to be a trifle severe with her, rather more than is expected from one who is merely reconstructing a historically unimportant person, and the remains take on the dimensions of life with disconcerting clearness: there she stands, in her incredible majesty, and Mr. Forster invites us to smile with him at the happy effect of his labors.

We do smile, of course; it is impossible not to, but with a slight sense of guilt. The humor is rather too easy, the object too remote. Not quite fiction—indeed, a fact. Not quite innocently comic, as balloon sleeves are. She suffered few jests at her expense in her living presence. Only one is recorded, and even on that occasion her moral victory was complete.

Mr. Forster gives her credit for her qualities, even though he cannot admire them. To view her through his balanced, observant and critical mind is to repeat in a measure the delight experienced in reading any other work of his; but even without his notes it is possible to reconstruct this obdurate, tough-souled creature, who gave her squalid fate a sturdy battle. She had a few real adventures, with no consolations outside herself and religion. Divine Providence was her spiritual stay, though she pulled through everything by main muscle. Born in a country where caste was life, she had no caste to speak of, and she had no husband worth mentioning in an age when a woman could scarcely survive without one. Yet she survived, and up to a point surmounted the difficulties of her sphere. The safely entrenched may despise such survivals, but Mrs. Fay came of a class that knew the need of tooth and claw.

It was survival by a series of failures. She failed at everything in the end—at marriage, at mantua making, at trade, at shipping. Because she was, after her fashion, an individualist, she got no help from people. When she was in prison in Calicut, someone sent her a teakettle. There was a feud between her and her fellow prisoners, and she meant to monopolize that teakettle. So they stole it from her. This in a sentence is the story of her life and her personal relations.

No doubt of it, hers was a solid and light-proof temperament. She modeled her style on phrases and her conduct on foregone conclusions. To those who traveled with her, she was a scorpion. Mostly persons of no consequence, like herself, she repelled them instinctively, for she had ambitions. When in her wanderings she encountered persons of good society, she fawned upon them. They in turn seemed to have treated her with pleasant condescension, for which she was properly grateful. Her sharp unsentimental middle-class eyes saw through the vanities of this world, nevertheless, and from time to time she records her moral conclusions upon society.

Numberless shrewd plans for getting on in the world failed, somehow, to come off. To the last she tussled along half-equipped, with not quite enough money, or imagination, or grammar. She traveled and scribbled and fought, and once came to legal troubles with a servant girl. The servant girl publicly accused her of misconduct with a ship's surgeon. This must have been a blow, but Mrs. Fay passed it over in dignified silence. She was strong on dignified silence. For nineteen years she kept her own counsel about the true cause of her separation from her husband, and even planned to educate his illegitimate child in England, but the ship on which he sailed was lost at sea. Her British sense of moral obligation and her female sense of moral injury never failed her. These combined with piety and rhetoric made her letters what they are. That they should not have been suffered to drop soundlessly into oblivion is merely the final absurd accident of her absurd fate.

They outlived her, having been preserved by her sister, to whom they were chiefly addressed. Later, in old age, Mrs. Fay needed money, as always. She wrote an autobiographical set-piece, patching out the record from memory to increase the volume to the fashionable weight of the day. She died, intestate and insolvent, before it could be published, and it finally came into print in the hope that its sale would benefit her creditors. Her creditors were not benefited, for the book passed almost unnoticed. It was waiting for Mr. Forster.

✍ Dora, the Dodo, and Utopia

New York Herald Tribune Books, November 8, 1925, p. 14.

Review of *Lysistrata, or Woman's Future and Future Woman*, by Anthony M. Ludovici (New York: E. P. Dutton and Company, 1924); and *Hypatia, or Woman and Knowledge*, by Mrs. Bertrand Russell (New York: E. P. Dutton and Company, 1925).

Utopias are steadily on the decline. Even Sir Thomas More could not imagine one that excluded capital punishment, human slavery and the custom of children standing behind their elders at table, waiting to be fed with scraps of food cold from the dishes. If, with all his prodigious equipment of erudition and humanity, Sir Thomas failed in dealing with crime, with labor and the proper care of children, how, then, can lesser minds venture so boldly in and present their pet little horrors as models for the future customs of the human race? Yet they continually do it, and write books about it, and too often find publishers.

Mr. Ludovici, beginning with a single idea, and that a fallacy, has created a whole set of airy worlds with god-like nonchalance and lack of forethought. He presents us with a past of which, I confess, I scarcely recognize a single feature. He sets before us a present which, I firmly believe, is at least half non-existent. And he offers us a choice of two futures, both based on impossibilities. The first is Utopia, and it depends on the complete supremacy of man over woman; the second, which he hardly dares to name, depends on the supremacy of woman over man.

Briefly, there was a time, says the author, taking refuge in pre-historic aeons, when men were lords of life and women were their cheerful, obedient dependents. On these terms love was ecstasy, health was perfect, there was no provoking feminist agitation or scientific tampering with the psyche. Of economic and political problems he says nothing, so we are happily to presume that they had not been invented. The decline of this natural supremacy of men over women, due to the unaccountable discontent of the women themselves, whom nothing can please, has brought man low and the world to its present unhealthful state. On this decline Mr. Ludovici blames the difficulties of parturition, the habitual wearing of glasses, the prevalence of bridgework in the mouth, the unsettled condition of society and the consequent popular use of digestive tablets.

The cure for all this, says Mr. Ludovici, lies in a mere resurgence of good, old-fashioned, romantic, hearty masculinity. Men must be so intelligent that the most intelligent women shall be as children beside them. They must be so entertaining that the women will willingly stay at home and listen to their conversations. They must be so strong willed that no woman can resist them, and such competent amorists that no woman can teach them anything.

The consequence of this brilliant program is, as you have guessed, Utopia, founded on the material and spiritual dependency of women, unlimited childbirth without the use of anaesthetics, a rigorous selection of the unfit for slaughter shortly after birth and a system of healing by faith and the laying on of hands. There are other conditions also, but these are the chief benefits that shall accrue to women in this ideal state.

If it occurs to the reader that this is mere childish nonsense, not worth repeating, I assure him that this booklet is a literary curiosity of genuine value and should be preserved as part of the records of our times. The outline of the alternate future, with women in the ascendant, is even more fantastic. But I cannot give it space.

Mr. Ludovici planned both of his futures without reckoning on Mrs. Dora Russell. This is a characteristic flaw. A round dozen like her would be sufficient to upset any future he might project. She is a direct descendant of that first pre-historic virago who turned a realistic eye upon her surroundings and perceived that a man standing between her and the world represented not so much defense, protection, entertainment and nourishment as a mere shutting out of light and air. Thus she sets out to demolish Mr. Ludovici and makes an extremely neat job of it. Her mind is young, resilient, combative, and many things annoy her. The things that annoy her most are Dodoism, represented by her opponent; sentimentality about sex and the insistent claim of a certain type of male to a supremacy he has never quite been able to establish.

Mrs. Russell is no academic debater. Her logic is straight, and her attack is direct. She is a born fighter and has sharpened her weapons on the grinding stone of immediate life. When she retreats into the past it is to drag forth old scores and call for a settlement. An understanding of the labor problem, political and economic conditions, the personal lives of modern women, especially working women, give her argument abundant vigor and relevancy. Psychologically she is perversely a bit of a martyr; a feminist or anybody else who has a long-standing grievance is apt to be. She offers no possible future not grounded in a present righting of human wrongs. Single-mindedness and a sense of reality, the special gifts of the intelligent virago, belong in a high degree to Mrs. Russell. Feminists should place a considerable value on her; and, considering that she speaks for a great number of them, Mr. Ludovici may well become more and more nervous about the future he built so neatly out of dreams.

✍ The Great Catherine

New York Herald Tribune Books, November 29, 1925, p. 3.

Review of *Catherine the Great,* by Katharine Anthony
(New York: Alfred A. Knopf, 1925).

Merely because this is a second book by a writer whose first was a masterpiece, I shall not follow my impulse and begin by comparing them. They claim my admiration on separate grounds, and I urge you to read them both, for I know of no better modern biographies than these two.

In *Margaret Fuller: A Psychological Biography* Miss Anthony proved herself a subtle explorer of souls by the psycho-analytic method. She chose a great subject in *Margaret Fuller* and her near kinship with that firm-textured spirit made interpretation a labor of love. Being pre-natally informed about everything that went into the life of the American woman, Miss Anthony wrote of her with an intimacy, a friendliness, that testified to many generations of nearness and understanding. So much for that book, which is a true act of creation and cannot be explained.

With modifications Miss Anthony has applied to the life story of Catherine the Great this same method of analysis, and again we have a book that marches full of glow and the substance of reality. Out of a monstrous legend she has brought her subject alive, has cleared away the debris from her name and has given to the work of clarifying the motives of Catherine the same considering scientific mind, the same ardor of truth that she devoted to Margaret Fuller. In her search she took nothing for granted, and she removed all labels from the woman before she began the work of reconstruction. To her it is nothing that Catherine is remembered as a great autocrat and a notorious wanton. These are results, and causes interest Miss Anthony. Catherine the Great was first of all a human being, born to common heritage of obscure complexities, worthy to be noted, because she presents a remarkable total of reactions to the circumstances of her life. In making her estimate Miss Anthony went straight to the sources and got at the truth by way of the subject's own confessions, in the way of psychologists.

The Empress of Russia was a prodigious pen-woman, especially frank, clear-headed and witty when she wrote down her thoughts. She left a library of her writings. Manifestoes, ukases, political pamphlets, correspondence with Voltaire and Grimm did not suffice to free her busy mind. Fragments of tales, legends written for her grandsons, two volumes of a history of Russia, comedies modeled on the style of Molière, all flowed from her inkwell. And most valuable of all, she wrote her memoirs, two sets of them, one in youth, one in age.

While in Russia Miss Anthony examined all these documents, long suppressed and only recently opened; with a keen eye for probabilities she separated fact from fantasy and picked her psychological clews unerringly from both. Taking firm hold of the thin mysterious line of secret life in this personality, she charts it clearly from the cradle of little Fike of Zerbst to the death bed of the Empress.

This line holds the wild cross currents of the story together and establishes the deep communication between early seemingly trivial episodes and their final result in the shape of terrific deeds. Even in such simple connections as the early poverty of the German Princess and her later extravagance as sovereign with gifts and honors, we are never permitted to lose sight of this hidden interplay of influences in her long progress of liberation. For liberation it was. She had manifold dangerous powers within her and finally she was strong enough to give them full play.

As a young simple German Princess she had an intelligent governess, Babet Cardel, who combatted the influences of ignorance around her pupil; a foggy-minded old Lutheran pastor undertook to nourish her soul. A half century later these two still contested for governorship in the memory of the Empress, but Babet Cardel seems to have triumphed by the record. Until she went to Russia to be married in her fifteenth year she was the mere shadow of her vain, nitwitted mother, who had the energy and the will to make schemes, but not the cleverness to make them go. Her father, pious, high-minded, abstract, was led about blindfolded by his wife. All around the child were dreadful spinster aunts full of strange habits and thwarted vainglory. She was the only normal child in a sick family, a household hag-ridden by poverty, baffled worldly aims and religious superstition. She was not beautiful, she seemed to have no personality, and she was dowerless.

Yet—her trip to Russia liberated her from her mother. Female despots in the making do not suffer from the mother fixation. She allied herself with the Empress Elizabeth in the early quarrels which developed between the two older women, but in her after life she ruled men as she had seen her mother rule her father. Her conversion to the Greek faith was a mere act of state, but it released her from the gloomy theology of Pastor Wagner. Her first lover, Saltikov, set her free from her husband and her nine years' servitude to a sterile marriage. It gave her the natural power of the mother of an heir to the throne. Her husband's indifference and her desertion by Saltikov wounded her female pride, hardened her heart. She deliberately asserted her will and her latent charm to reassure herself of her own value. She gained a victory of cajolery over the Empress Elizabeth, who taxed her with high treason during the Seven Years' War with Prussia. Catherine stood her ground unaided, and nothing was proved against her, though every one else implicated in the plot was lost. She learned by this her power of getting the loyalty of men; it gave her a certain measure of her skill at secret diplomacy and her resources in a crisis.

In the end she deposed her husband, seized his throne over the rights of her son as direct heir, and shielded her husband's murderers by announcing he had died of a colic in prison. She put through the partition of Poland, recast into a fixed code the weltering Russian laws, gained Crimea and Georgia for Russia, and became Catherine the Great by acclaim of her subjects. Never again was she unsuccessful with lovers. She used them up and weaned them off, and they went away to various melodramatic ends, some to obscurity, some to madness, others to death. Her final estimate of herself, no doubt a true one, was that she was fond of reading, was "good natured and easy going" and "loved sociability and the arts." "I have an unbridled temerity," she also said of herself. She had indeed, for she broke a dynasty, and set a Saltikov on the throne of Russia, and made her subjects believe he was a Romanov. Miss Anthony casually sets history straight here and there as she goes. She reduces many tumid tales to life size, and reveals the natural faces of the main characters of Catherine the Great's drama. Potiomkin, the Empress Elizabeth, the Countess Dashkov, Gregory Orlov, all are presented acutely, and there is not a first rate soul or intelligence among them. Catherine bore the enormous loneliness of an intelligent sovereign in a court of nobles who were almost as ignorant as her peasants. The grandeur of their dress did not blind her to their filth, their dirty cold palaces, their stupidity, their craftiness. She had three fears: she feared venereal disease, smallpox and ignorance. She had three thirsts: to enlighten her people, to liberate her own mind through science and literature, and to extend the boundaries of Russia.

The partition of Poland was the first outcropping of this predatory instinct, the natural accompaniment of her love of all possessions. "Because she had come without sheets to Russia," says Miss Anthony, "she was obliged to put through the partition of Poland." She was the ringleader, abetted by Frederick of Prussia and Maria Theresa of Austria. Catherine the Great was delightfully catty about Maria Theresa—she was in general not fond of women—calling her the "dear worthy Lady Prayerful," yet she took uneasy note of her, as the Empress Elizabeth did before her. The fecund Austrian Queen was an occasion of gall to these ambitious women, who between them had shunted three generations of weak-kneed children into state marriages, with most discouraging results. It has been argued that Frederick the Great led in the Polish business, but Miss Anthony here establishes that Catherine went first, with Frederick at her heels, and the pious but greedy Maria Theresa coming in for her share without actually putting her hands in the pitch.

Catherine the Great used her human material about her in whatever form it came. She despised Maria Theresa, but connived with her. She put her Polish lover Poniatovsky on the throne of Poland, and he stayed there as long as it served her purpose. She forgot about him afterward. Even against her enemies she seemed to have no rancors, being too strong to bear grudges, and having no need for them. There were always about her, solidly devoted to her, lesser wits who would bear grudges in her stead, and, if need be, do her killing for her. She usually chose her lovers for their good looks, but three or four of them were useful to her in practical ways.

Her erotic legend is robust: she is credited with three hundred lovers. Miss Anthony has devoted only one chapter to this part of her life, and has picked her way carefully among the thousand obscene and comic stories of which the Empress is the heroine in Russia even to this day. We are reminded that the Empress Elizabeth and the mother of Sergei Saltikov also were said to have had three hundred lovers. It is the classic number, attached to the names of many heroines of amour, among them Ninon De L'Enclos. As a matter of record, by her own confession to Potiomkin, Catherine the Great had twelve lovers, and her husband, who need not be counted. She named them all, and dated them, in her letter. She had no casual intrigues. Her lover was an affair of state. She selected her favorite—they grew younger and younger as she grew older and older, but this, too, is in the classic tradition—and named him adjutant general. He was given gorgeous clothes, an apartment, and put on a liberal salary. But first he was examined by the court physician, and then turned over for an apprenticeship to two ladies of the court. If he survived he became, as one of them, Vassilchikov, complained, "nothing more than a kept woman, and was treated as such." This Vassilchikov was a failure, even after all the precautions, so no wonder he complained.

The Empress sent him away, and took the famous Potiomkin. He was an old friend, he had helped her to seize the throne. She loved him for fifteen years, and shared her dreams of driving the Turk out of Europe with him. They went on the fantastic pilgrimage into the Crimea together. He was the chief of her three trusted generals.

From the time of Potiomkin's pitiable death by the roadside the

Empress waned into resistant old age, and into a sprawling, ignomin-
ious death, and from the grave she came back, but not as Matushka,
the Little Mother, as she called herself, not as the woman who had
loved Russia and the arts, who had the force and will to change the
history of Europe. No. She passed into the popular annals of her
adopted country as the heroine of half its broad stories, as a woman
who painted her face and smelt of snuff and took three hundred lovers
with the hearty gusto of a female dragoon.

Miss Anthony notes that this would have delighted Catherine the
Great; for she wished to be remembered as victorious. And she knew
her world thoroughly. Time has reduced her personality to a few
broad, easily legible, highly colored strokes, because the truth about
her is so intricate, and her failure so great.

✍ Mr. George on the Woman Problem

New York Herald Tribune Books, November 29, 1925, p. 11.

Review of *The Story of Women*, by W. L. George (New York:
Harper and Brothers, 1925).

Years ago, when I was badly upset over the fact that women enjoyed no suffrage at the ballot box, it annoyed me grievously to hear
Mr. W. L. George referred to as a friend of women; as a man who
understood women, at that. Suspicious by temperament, as I was of
those who professed loyalty to our Great Cause even though by birth
they belonged to the opposite camp, doubly suspicious of men who
made a business of understanding women, and endlessly suspicious
of gentlemen authors who wrote slick, patronizing articles about us
for the syndicated press, I rejected the good offices of Mr. George and
repudiated his ideas about us.

Time has confirmed this adolescent judgment. Book after book
about the ladies have we suffered from Mr. George, and he has not
learned yet that we are not a problem. He belongs to that school
of male feminist who espouses the cause of woman. He feels that

it must be protected, guided, criticized, restrained within bounds of reason, saved from itself, flattered, exploited and occasionally betrayed. Betweenwhiles, it must be regarded as the subject of amateur laboratory experiment. The result is, or should be, a divorce.

But let's glance at the book. *The History of Women,* then, is a disconnected, rather fragmentary compilation, purposing to trace the progress of the female out of the pre-historic dark into the present filtering light of day. It is fairly accurate in historical data. Mr. George has read widely, if not deeply, among the endless writings of other men on this subject. Considering the enormous body of evidence which already exists, it was hardly worth while to add this uninspired bit of hackwork.

Skipping jauntily from age to age, he discovers that woman, the problem, has ever been a slave, and even in our recent emancipation (his own word) he can see nothing particularly solid or promising. He notes, from time to time, that such freedom as she has gained is not due to her own efforts, but is a practical result of the growing advancement and increasing human benevolence of man. The further advancement of woman depends on the developing generosity of man, for, as heretofore, she must continue to find her true channel of expression through him.

This is moldy stuff, indeed. The woman problem has found a husband in Mr. George.

✍ Etiquette in Action

New York Herald Tribune Books, December 20, 1925, p. 13.

Review of *Parade: A Novel of New York Society,* by Emily Post (New York: Funk and Wagnalls Company, 1925).

Mrs. Post has been for long an excellent liaison officer between New York society and that great formless indiscriminate welter, the population of the United States of America. Hers has been no sinecure. On the one side she has been an authoritative arm upholding tribal usage and observance. A lifelong familiarity with that vast canon has sensitized her to its most subtle nuances. She has become the high priestess of good manners, expounding the Scriptures even in the temples of the most high.

On the other side, hers has been an apostolic mission. She carries the word to the population, and is at once the interpreter and apologist—in the classic sense of that noble word—of society. Her recent textbook, *Etiquette*, was a godsend to more than one poor lamb born outside the fold; and now, after a proper interval for absorption and meditation on those invaluable rules of conduct, *Parade* appears, showing etiquette in action on her own ground, kicking her train, spooning her soup, putting down presumptuous persons, presiding at charity bazaars, giving entertainments, living her private life in fact.

The invaluable personal idiom and point of view of Mrs. Post presents to us a New York social atmosphere breathing of innocent, self-conscious swish. Its members are, or were, unanimous in carrying on a naïve tradition of gentility, a chatty noblesse oblige. They never forget the estate to which it has pleased God to call them, and they are as thrilled over being well-bred as if it had happened only yesterday.

Their sense of solidarity is simply noble, there is no other word for it. We note that a young British marquis, during the war, dashes off immediately to get a commission, "like all of the other aristocrats." Similar incidents will be remembered even on this side. Their social reserve in discussing scandal is perfect: "I don't think I'd trust even a statue with Bronson," says one gentleman to another during one of these Arabian Nights fêtes. "There are probably lots of his type in the world, but he is the only one whose wreckage I have personally seen. Nelly Keith was as free from any trace of moral laxity as one could be until Bronson made love to her. She's still up at Dr. Gaylord's sanatorium in Greenville. . . ."

But Nelly Keith is not the heroine. No such crass fate befalls Geraldine Loring. She is of good family, but poor, and she has no illusions about love. She wants luxury, social prestige. For these she jilts her faithful but penniless love, and marries a young man named

Ollie, member of one of New York's first families. He gets slightly pie-eyed during the wedding feast, but in a nice way, of course, and as she is a chill, unawakened maiden, he reads detective stories during the first lap of the honeymoon.

Geraldine, who is frankly dust-colored, decides to become a beauty. This she does almost overnight by means of a dash of dye on the eyelashes, a henna-gold hair wash, and some discreetly compounded face creams. For the next quarter of a century she devotes her energies to preserving the beauty thus wantonly acquired. It rewards her with the illicit attentions of the dangerous Bronson, bent on personally making of her another wreckage. Her husband comes into the drawing room, finds her sitting in indiscreet proximity to this fascinating fiend. What can a gentleman in good society do at such a crisis? He blows out his so-to-speak brains, and leaves the beauteous Geraldine a repentant widow. She casts the wrecker out of her life and goes on with her facial massage and beauty diets.

All the other matrons of her generation are immersed in really worthwhile activities, charity work, committee meetings and social service. Not so Geraldine. Just as she has reached the peak of her synthetic beauty, the war comes along and spoils everything. She loses most of her fortune and she does not dash with the other ladies into beautifully tailored uniforms and war-work. The helter-skelter of the times breaks down all the barricades. The newly rich climbers come stampeding in, and Geraldine faces the great crisis of her life when she discovers that in her early climbing days she had snubbed all the wrong people. The snubbed ones had by no means gone away and died, but had gone on climbing over some one else, and now at last she finds them sitting in places to which even she had not aspired.

There is nothing to do but cultivate them a little, which she does, and finds hearts of gold beating under these over decorated bosoms. Besides, they all learn quickly, and shortly they are scarcely distinguishable from the elect.

Even her old love betrays her by becoming a great, mysterious hero, sketchily similar to young Lawrence in Arabia, and falling in love

with Ambrosia Jimpson, now widow of a marquis, daughter of a vege-
table canning creature whom Geraldine has disregarded long since.

As time goes on, she gets hazier and hazier about everything. Never
above the average in intelligence, she swoons mentally under the
strain. She loses all, including her good looks, and becomes a bel-
dame as inexplicably as she became a beauty. The younger generation
takes to drink and cabaret life before her very eyes, and the genteel
society of New York seems in rather a bad way, as the story bows
itself out. The moral appears to be that Literature and Etiquette make
bad bed-fellows.

✍ Ay, Que Chamaco

New Republic, vol. 45, no. 577 (December 23, 1925), pp. 141–42.

Review of *The Prince of Wales and Other Famous Americans*. Caricatures by
Miguel Covarrubias (New York: Alfred A. Knopf, 1925).

In Mexico there is a well seasoned tradition of fine caricature: almost
every one of the younger painters possesses this lacerating gift. It
goes with the Mexican aptitude for deadly discernment of the comic
in the other person, together with each man's grave regard for his
own proper dignity. In arguments, whether personal or political, they
resort early to popular songs and cartoons that carry sharper fangs
than any other sort of debate. They have a charming habit of disregarding the main point at issue long enough to call attention to some
defect or weakness, preferably an irremediable one, in the opponent.
The quick-witted public, humanly fond of a joke on someone else,
laughs the loser out.

Covarrubias in this is more Mexican than the Mexicans. As a youth
he moved among that group of younger insurgents who revolution-
ized Mexican painting almost overnight. He was the youngest, and no
one was ever born so naïve as he appeared. He did no serious painting,
but amused himself at the innocent pastime of making caricatures of

the serious paintings of others, and thereafter it was an effort to look at those paintings with an untangled viewpoint. He had a merry little way of dropping into the cafés haunted by his set, joining the carefree group gathered there, and dashing off a few careless impressions of their faces that would spoil their evening for them.

While he was yet too young to be called to account, he brought his talents to New York, and for once the favorite success legend of this nation jibed with the pure truth. The brilliant suddenness of his popularity made the old-fashioned tales of the hardships of genius sound a trifle drab, as his caricature of our native celebrities put a crimp in the high seriousness of intellectual life as she was being led in this city.

Smart New York, under whose garment of custom tailored sophistication beats an eager barbarian heart, touched to wonder by all that is deft, off-hand and of high visibility, had found a new champion; a boy with sure-fire stuff, backed up with the invaluable social gift of malice. "Enfant du siècle" they dubbed him, among other things. He is more than a mere child of his century; more than contemporaneous. He is current—as aptly present in the public interest as this month's leading musical revue.

It is his speed, his wit, his lively accuracy that first arrest the attention. But beyond his showy technique he has the spontaneous combustion called genius. In this collection of more than sixty drawings, there is only one failure: Babe Ruth. And that merely a comparative failure. There are less than half a dozen that are not superb. The rest are beyond criticism as keen satirical comment, and I claim it is a comment considerably more than skin-deep.

Covarrubias has a wide range of symbols, a command of many styles, and he adapts his medium and his method of approach with an impish understanding of the personality of his subject. Compare the caricatures of Alfred Stieglitz, of Calvin Coolidge, of Robert Edmond Jones, of Xavier Algara. If in the case of President Coolidge he has subtly piled up the miserable details, at other times he strips his subject to the buff: literally, in the drawing of Jack Dempsey, where in a few strokes we are given three dimensions, a framework with a skeleton inside: and in all of them, something else that belongs to metaphysics: a feeling that he has exposed the very outer appearance of a sitter that is the clue to an inner quality the sitter has spent most of his life trying to hide, or disguise. If that isn't murder, what is it? And what is?

The victims in Mexico used to shake their heads, to get the blood out of their eyes, no doubt. There, let a good joke get out on you just once, and you're done for. Their civilized perception of the power of wit makes for caution. "Ay, que chamaco!" they would say. "What a brat!" They preserved the drawings he made of them on scraps of paper around café tables, and if they were published, what a book that would be! But they will never be published. New York knows a good joke on itself when it sees it: and Covarrubias is the latest, and the best one.

✎ A Singing Woman

New York Herald Tribune Books, April 18, 1926, p. 6.

Review of *Words for the Chisel,* by Genevieve Taggard
(New York: Alfred A. Knopf, 1926).

In reading this collection of poems by Genevieve Taggard I am not reminded of Blake, though the slipcover encourages me to recall him in order better to appreciate certain subtleties of the newer poet. I much prefer to concentrate on these poems without a distracting search for comparisons. *Words for the Chisel* need not be compared with anything else; this is poetry, to be read for its own sake, and the reader need not fear he shall be made uneasy by reminiscence or deafened by echoes.

This poet has music and emotion and distinction of utterance. With her uncommon capacity for feeling she might have run away into sheer formlessness; with sober courage she has disciplined her instrument to the precise uses of her gift. Titles are often misleading; this one is not. At her best Miss Taggard carves in granite. At

her worst—or rather least—she models in honest clay. This present
volume is far above her first, *For Eager Lovers,* and there is no reason
to believe she has reached her full power.

This growth is accompanied by a strengthening of fiber. If her
battle with the invisible powers continues too rigorously or is too
much prolonged she is in danger of turning to stone.

But this is preferable to the lush over-ripeness into which her
warm, color-loving soul might have betrayed her. For nineteen years
she lived in Hawaii, near the sea; these poured their riches into
the veins of her youth. Even now this memory, this stored warmth,
softens the edges of her images, gives radiance to her words. Without
this beginning she might have lost her natural ardency, for there is
nothing here to preserve in a poet any sure faith in the testimony of
his own emotions; but her instincts have been but little blunted, and
she is a natural singing woman.

> Ethereal energy, airy lust,
> Intangible madness—these have made
> A bee-like cloud above her head.
>
> The coward, the coward is running home,
> To hide herself in a bed of dust—
> To huddle into an ugly bed.
> Underground they can never come.
>
> She broke and ate their honeycomb.
> Over her belly the bees will hum.

I have been looking through this book trying to discover why it
has created in my mind a world clear yet stained all through with
color; not glittering jewel colors, but the natural brightness of the
sky and the wet greenness of wild foliage. I cannot lay hold of a line
or passage that does it completely; still, the effect grows and glows
more vividly as poem follows poem. I get a sense of vast distances,
of clear, deep waters and the wild, hurrying spaces of the sky. Yet
Miss Taggard is in no sense concerned objectively with nature and is
no dallier with pantheism. I think she identifies human beings with

trees because in her natural right mood they seem fairly the same thing to her:

> A crowd of women like a little wood
> Of barefoot birches running under oaks.
> Wait on the hillside, linger, old and young,
> This being spring and trouble in their blood.

Miss Taggard has been called a feminist. As a term used to describe a poet, this word seems quite meaningless. She is "modern" in the sense that she belongs to her time, and therefore does not assume female poses merely pleasing to the eye. Nowhere in the poetry of women of other times do we find, save in one or two instances, any honest utterance about the true nature of love. Miss Taggard assumes no poses whatever; love is for her a terrific experience of the flesh that takes a wounding toll of the spirit; she addresses herself with superb directness to the lover as a sharer of the catastrophe. She stands up to a hand-to-hand battle, she wrestles with her angel: "I will not let thee go except thou bless me!" Being neo-pagan she is in no doubt as to the nature of the struggle, and refuses the dishonest shelter of sublimated tenderness or of the mother instinct.

The finest poems in this book are not love poems at all, in the lyrical sense. "Poppy Juice" is a long drama of nostalgia; it is quietly, deeply told, the thrill of horror at the last is almost whispered. And it ends in a clear serenity; after the strain and stress there is a sense of triumph in the folded hands and the relaxed voice. This characteristic quiet is not always triumph:

> There being pain for tasting Paradise
> And pain for lack of it: pain twice:
>
> And the last pain: to see the flying moon
> To be immobile and to make no moan.

These are the last two couplets of "Dissonance Then Silence," my choice among the shorter poems, in spite of "Truce" and "Elegy in Dialogue." In this second poem the poet approaches death and examines the mute threatening thing with bitter curiosity. "Long Dialogue" and "Threnody in Thin Air" have a true unearthly quality of singing, it is the "voice in the cloud" that spins and hums in slow somersaults of rapture. "Words for the Chisel" begins with feet solidly on earth, and rises through stones and trees and waters to the upper air, to a quiet, un-urgent end:

> Listen to the voice
> In the cloud
> Listen to the loud
> And suddenly ended
> Outcry
> It is my
> Voice in the high
> Moon-running ruin of the sky
>
> If you will not listen
> If you are afraid
> I will go higher
> Where you will not hear

✐ History for Boy and Girl Scouts

New Republic, vol. 48, no. 623 (November 10, 1926), p. 353.

Review of *Daniel Boone: Wilderness Scout*, by Stewart Edward White (New York: Doubleday, Page, and Company, 1926).

Before reviewing this book, I should have shown it to an intelligent child of ten: taking my lead from his comment, I should be sure of making no mistakes. Living as I do among frostbitten adults, with frost sitting upon my own head, how shall I, a respectable admirer of children, venture what literature is "good" for the young? At the age of twelve, I read *Alice in Wonderland* with joy, but I also got a power of good out of a stray copy of Rabelais. In that day there were no Boy and Girl Scouts, likewise no entertaining history of Daniel Boone. Now there are both, purely designed for each other. Early I was told by history books that Boone, a God-fearing misanthrope, opened the Wilderness Trail into Kentucky, the dark and bloody ground. I knew better, because my grandmother told me better, but the whole picture of Daniel Boone presented to me was singularly unattractive. He had the disadvantage of being somewhat in the family, and his coon-skin cap and God-fearingness annoyed me.

Since reading this book by Mr. Stewart Edward White I feel better. Daniel Boone, wilderness scout, comes alive without the prunes of moral or the prisms of hero-worship. The story has the virtues of clear writing, historical correctness and even of symbolic truth: for if the legend of Boone has grown somewhat disproportionate, it is well to remember that these tales were remembered and told by his contemporaries. If it is not wise always to accept a man at the valuation placed on him in his own lifetime, it is not much wiser to reject it altogether later on.

It is clear that we shall have few legends left after the realistic-minded amateur historians have done with our national past: I tremble for Poetry and Patriotism, those twin forces that create a national culture. But no doubt the future has other plans and they will not be missed. Mr. White feels tenderly about legends: anxiously he seeks to preserve this homespun epic for the young. After examining carefully the documentary evidence, he has thrown away little of the old material: we read of log raisings, quilting bees, backwoods weddings that enliven the hardships, the Indian raids and the tortures endured with equanimity by uniformly heroic women and strong men. He describes their background, and it is easy to believe that only the adventurous, the foolhardy, or the desperate would have been in such a place. One chapter especially pleased me: quite a full account of the pioneer fire-arms, their bullets and powder horns, their equipment and technique of marksmanship. The author takes pains to explode James Fenimore Cooper's painstaking inaccuracies, he speaks severely of plain and fancy liars. Daniel Boone is not magnified beyond life-size: he becomes a reasonable hero, and so does Simon Kenton. The Indians, too, are humanized; any fair-minded child will at once see their side of the story.

The book is very handsome, large and well bound, with a thin clear type. If the pictures are beautifully reproduced, and in brilliant colors, they also confuse me a little: the design seems too sophisticated even for children. How am I to judge? I buy only those books for children illustrated by Pamela Bianco. Pictures or not, boys and girls will probably like this story, because it is a thrilling yarn, told with zest, and the author has resisted pointing a moral until the very tag-end. Even then he does not take unfair advantage of his reader, but tacks it on in a paragraph by itself, where any quick-witted child may spot it at a glance: and so close the book.

✍ Enthusiast and Wildcatter

New York Herald Tribune Books, February 4, 1927, p. 14.

Review of *The City of the Sacred Well*, by T. A. Willard
(New York: Century Company, 1926).

Whereas, nearly all the really desirable ruins in other parts of the world have long since been staked off by duly authorized archaeologists working with some important museum or scientific society, Mexico has been until recently a very heaven for the wildcatter.

Now the Carnegie Expedition is in Yucatan, well established, and Dr. Manuel Gamio is (or was, the last I heard—things change so!) well in command of the archaeological and ethnological situation in the central plateau. This has put the kibosh on those delightful oldtime prospectors who used to take a mule train and a few Indian guides and hit the trail looking for buried cities.

My good friend William Niven, in the last half-century or so, has found so many remains I can't pretend to name them without my notebooks; but I know he dug up treasure and gave much of it to the National Museum of Mexico. Latterly he developed theories—having been made Fellow in a great number of geographical and scientific societies—and you never heard such theories, so fascinating they could not well be true. All sorts of important explorer-scientists—

Dr. Spinden, Dr. Morley, dear knows who else—used to come and look at his stuff and speculate informally on origins. Niven put all these random speculations together with all his own ideas, and what a story they did make!

A notable Mexican archaeologist fought him fiercely as a menace to science. Niven loved this, egged him on, and enlisted some very solid friends on his side. The archaeologist was wrong to accuse Niven of making ruined cities by hand and burying them himself, and then hiring Indians to dig them up again, because it was so manifestly impossible that Niven could do it, even if he had wanted to, he being then about seventy-eight years old. Still, it all goes to show how these enthusiasts, these finders, can drive a scientific and considering man out of his mind, for they clutter up the scene, and dig out of hours, and go about hooting with joy, getting their names in the papers and writing books that are merely smoke screens.

Which brings me somewhat to the case of Edward H. Thompson, archaeologist and researcher, born enthusiast and wildcatter, who has spent thirty years unearthing the secrets of ancient Yucatan. True, Mr. Thompson went to Mexico under impeccable auspices, in the double rôle of American Consul and unofficial investigator for the American Antiquarian Society and the Peabody Museum of Harvard. He has worked faithfully with several regularly organized expeditions, but he was never happier than when he was going alone, and his best work has been done when he had "only his faithful native followers." He discovered ruined cities, carried on research in others already discovered, and at last crowned his labors by dredging up the treasure from the Sacred Well of Chichen-Itza, where the Mayas used to cast a living maid, together with precious metals and jewels, during their yearly ceremony of propitiation to the Rain God.

His story, a gorgeous jumble of fact and fancy, personal adventure, odd scraps of history and legend, together with his own notions, has been written down by T. A. Willard; it makes a readable book, and in those parts that relate directly his own experience, a valuable book. No other man will dredge that well. In this his experience is unique; he may well glorify it in a tale. But alas! Mr. Thompson feels there may be something in the legend that the Mayas are one of the lost tribes of Israel. There may be something in the Lost Atlantis legend, too: he has it on various good authorities that all sorts of wild ideas are hard facts, and the reader is befogged with speculations.

In the mean time the publicity end of the Carnegie Expedition gets out long-winded solemn pieces about the true state of affairs in Yucatan, the true state appearing to be that there is nothing much new to add; they are getting there an inch at a time, and when anything really happens we shall hear of it. It is hard to be breezy and popular and full of news and exact at the same time—everybody knows that. So for the moment the diggers, those gay enthusiasts and fearless pioneers, have the stories mostly to themselves.

People will read a lively, scrambling yarn like this, where the main interest is a human one. If what the man did is exciting enough, who cares what he thinks? If the scientific part of this book is not of much importance, the personal story of Edward Thompson is: like Niven, with his own hands he has brought enough mystery out of Mexican earth to keep the scientists busy racking their brains for twenty years.

✍ Black, White, Red, Yellow and the Pintos

New Republic, vol. 1, no. 641 (March 16, 1927), pp. 111–12.

Review of *The Ipané*, by R. B. Cunninghame Graham (New York: Albert and Charles Boni, 1925); *Doughty Deeds, an Account of the Life of Robert Graham of Gartmore, Poet and Politician, 1735–1797*, by R. B. Cunninghame Graham (New York: Dial Press, 1925); and *A Brazilian Mystic, Being the Life and Miracles of Antonio Conselheiro*, by R. B. Cunninghame Graham (New York: Dial Press, 1925).

Mr. Cunninghame Graham belongs to that very select, brave company of true adventurers who share in common a noble curiosity

about the life of man. By adventurers I don't mean soldiers, nor mis-
sionaries, nor politicians, nor reformers of any sort. I leave out, too,
all peripatetic prophets, tourists and journalists with one eye on the
public: I mean freemen, who go for love into the—to them—strange
corners of the world, with no ambitions to serve, and no job to do
that could bias the record they made. You see the list narrows: I have
in mind at this moment Doughty, and Burton and Hudson, who belong roughly to one period; there were a few before and there will be
a few more afterward, and in the meantime there is Cunninghame
Graham.

I don't know what it is, deep down, that makes the true adventurer.
They don't run in a pattern; I never heard of any two alike. They do
and think and feel vastly different things: they can't be accounted
for merely on the score of humanity and intelligence and curiosity.
There is something else in a man that invites him to hazards and
uncertainties for the sake of universal citizenship. They see straight,
and their records are the only ones I trust. Being, nearly all of them,
a blend of scholar, scientist and poet, their writing is not, profession-
ally speaking, literary. It is odd to think of Cunninghame Graham
regularly writing books; he is so little the dedicated litterateur. In
spite of his developed and definite style, you need to be reminded
that he comes of a fine old scribbling family.

Laird Nicol of Gartmore, that fell old carle, father of Doughty
Deeds, was the author of that famous pamphlet, *An Inquiry into the
Causes Which Facilitate the Rise and Progress of Rebellions and In-
surrections in the Highlands of Scotland* (1747), a source of reference
for Sir Walter Scott when he wrote Waverley, and Rob Roy. Robert
Graham of Gartmore wrote good letters and a set of verses called,
"If Doughty Deeds My Lady Please," and got his family nickname
by them. This Doughty Deeds Graham was a comfortably tough-
skinned, tender-hearted, moral-minded and loose-living gentleman:
he gave political allegiance to England, cultural obeisance to France,
but his true love to Jamaica, that island where he passed his youth in
a nice balance between the dissipations natural to his age and time,
and the making of a career for himself. Withal he was Scotch and

liberal, quite an eighteenth century product. He must have had wits and loveableness—I confess they are not clearly shown in this book. His portraits are against him, a pompous, roundish, squirish man with a ruddled eye and billowing chin. He tippled with Sheridan, and swapped political letters with Pitt, his idol and leader; provided for some, at least, of his Jamaican bastards, tenderly loved his fragile Creole wife, and was refreshingly free from pretense of any sort. His famous poem goes in the hard gallop that was the proper metre of the day. It is very doughty in its sentiments indeed, and he wrote it, probably for his own amusement, when he was lingering in his fifties. He was a reasonable man who knew the blight of logic when carried too far, and never connected his gout with his indulgence in port and rum. Thus he remained a pillar of the humanities until the end, leaving good memories and sound descendants. Still I prefer the grim old Laird, his father.

Now, as you read this book, there is a shadowy overlay of resemblance between these two and their descendant as he writes about them. Nothing tangible; it is in essence merely: but Cunninghame Graham can be placed; you feel there is a good accounting for him all along this vanished host of Scotch hard-heads and poets. He has a deliciousness of mind that they lacked, and that freedom which comes of having early got hold of the key of the world. He has been almost everywhere, and everything has had a meaning and an interest for him. "Still man exists, black, white, red, yellow and the Pintos of the State of Vera Cruz." He has got acquainted with enough of each kind and color to discover their under-the-skin likenesses and differences, and he tells of them not as if they were shows put on for his special amusement, but as human creatures that need not be hated, or despised, or feared, or improved.

I don't know if *The Ipané* is his first book. The preface makes me think it is, and the date is 1899. The contents, too, have that air of being snatched from the four winds and tied loosely together in a book. He has written short pieces about South America, Iceland, Arabia, Scotland, even Texas (just think, Texas was a foreign land to him!) and they have a rushing style; but there is time to put in everything: sidelights and scraps of information most travelers forget to add, so that when you see their country for the first time you are amazed at all they left out. There is this about these stories: you feel that the writer was a participant, not a looker-on. He tells what he knows.

In his story of Antonio Maciel, later called the Councillor, Mr. Graham has depended on Brazilian historians for his story, but creates the setting from his own knowledge of the country. It is a tale of religious frenzy and marvel that belongs, so you feel, to any age but this.

About thirty-five years ago, the mad prophet Antonio Conselheiro was killed, and his followers driven from his holy city in the desert, after a long siege by Brazilian government troops. His beginnings were simple. He married young, his wife deceived him with many men, and finally went away with one of them. Antonio bungled his case, thrashed a relative of the seducer and was sent to prison for a long term. He escaped and disappeared for ten years, and returned, emaciated, purified, in the garb of an anchorite.

To note that he is a marvelous subject for psychiatry is beside the point: almost everybody is. Mr. Graham tells his story without excursions into the new science, and thus considered, Antonio Conselheiro holds his own very well among the saints. He seems to have had the fervor of a Savonarola, without the senseless hatred and fury, and disciples flocked to him. At first, there were only outcasts, the simple, and women. Later came vaqueiros, lusty armed men on horseback, robbers and desperados of all sorts. It is curious to follow the history of a sect in the making, when the leader is sincere: seeing how a man, burning in his own fire, communicates that fire to others, where it burns to a different purpose and intent, so that they must lay down rules for the control of it. He became a saint to them, and the head of a schismatic sect—for they were all nominally Roman Catholic—they endured all persecutions and took to the Sertão, an almost impassable desert, and built themselves a city. His spiritual power over his city of ruffians grew until Church and State feared him, though he never concerned himself with their affairs, and they sent four bodies of soldiers, one after another, to reduce him. The chronicle of these sieges is too good to be mangled in re-telling. It is quite simply one of the best tales I have ever read. I think it must be superbly told, for I forgot the writing in the story.

✐ Paternalism and the Mexican Problem

New York Herald Tribune Books, March 27, 1927, p. 12.

Review of *Some Mexican Problems,* by Moises Saenz and Herbert I. Priestley (Chicago: University of Chicago Press, 1926); and *Aspects of Mexican Civilization,* by José Vasconcelos and Manuel Gamio (Chicago: University of Chicago Press, 1926).

I shall not pretend that these books present unbiased opinions of conclusions on the problem of Mexican-American relations, for liberalism has a bias of its own. The main virtue of the liberal temperament is its almost pious regard for the facts, its genius for patient research: for me, the wonder of the liberal temperament is that no amount of findings can upset its preconceived theories. Earth hath no sorrows that a firm mild course of popular education cannot cure.

It is true that ill-regimented minded are inclined to be noisy, warm and argumentative, and there is something about the Mexican question that raises the hackles even on the peaceful minded. These admirable books contain all the elements of free-for-all controversy, but all is so adroitly smoothed away there is nothing in the tone to frighten the most timid liberal. Four diverse, informed and civilized minds have here collaborated in presenting quite horrifying facts in an almost painless form. In this series of lectures they tested their theories of education before the Chicago Annual Institute, and it is cheerful to think that hundreds, maybe even thousands of students went away from there happy in the thought that nations may be taught understanding of each other by gentle degrees, as children are led from one grade to another. Even oil magnates may be taught international good manners by suggestion. In this thought everybody may happily go to sleep and leave the job of teaching them to some one else.

Each of these four gentlemen is an expert in his subject, a fine flower of academic culture. They share an Olympian balance in viewing all sides of a question. If at times Mr. Saenz shows fight he controls himself quickly, remembers his rôle of mediator, and gives a superhumanly just statement of the present intolerable situation in Mexico due to foreign investments, the condition of Mexican labor and the problem of rural education. He is a nationalist, a good one, I should like to hear him speak more freely. But he remains well within the bounds of what is expected from a foreign lecturer before an institute, and ends on a note of optimism scarcely warranted by the facts he has managed to expose. I suspect him of radical tendencies. Given a chance, I believe he would be warm and noisy. The balance of his head is threatened by the insurgence of his heart.

Mr. Vasconcelos, former secretary of education in Mexico, has for some years past occupied himself with promoting peaceful relationship between the Latin countries of America. He is equally opposed to the present system of government in these countries—dictatorship or caudillism—and foreign interference. He professes faith, more especially in the Mexican Indian, and rejects alien paternalism, but preaches a vast religious native paternalism fully as debilitating to his people. Mr. Vasconcelos has an incurable, almost romantic faith in the perfectibility of human nature, and his plan roughly is this: the lion and the lamb have essential differences, it is true, but one should reason with the lion and persuade him not to eat the lamb. In the meantime, the lamb shall be given a few setting up exercises that will enable him to hold his own with the lion in case one or the other of these essential differences should crop up in their future together.

Aside from this he gives an excellent historical survey of Mexico.

Into Mr. Priestley's scholarly essay creeps now and again his sense of responsibility as big brother of Mexico. He, with the others, is pleased that the Ford and the phonograph are now commonplaces of Mexican life. He believes in sane, conservative propaganda for Mexico, such as these books represent, setting aside all the roaring of distempered radicals and frivolous reports by prosperous Chamber of Commerce gentlemen. Truth being, of course, our aim, I only wish that these honest men and good investigators could manage to be half so entertaining as the liars and hotheads. There must be some way of making facts attractive! Why do not these liberals find it?

In his first chapter Mr. Priestley is gloomy as death about sickness in Mexico. But this, he says, is being remedied. Sanitary measures are being enforced, active steps taken against contagion and infection, a study of regional diseases promises a cure of them. These things are good, who could quarrel with them? But they continually miscall this sort of thing civilization. Maybe it is, and I am thinking of something else: I am persuaded it is too tall a name for our cult of machinery and the bathtub. Still the standard of washing and eating in Mexico remains very low.

The average of washing and eating in the United States is, as you know, unnaturally high. We have our bread lines, true, and miners' strikes, and the garment workers of this superlatively clothed nation have a permanent grievance, and the silk manufacturers will tell you that if we wear silk, even at excessive prices, a certain number of workers must live in acute discomfort. In the South we persist in the aristocratic old tradition, of Negro peonage, and there is a discouraging percentage of poor whites whose insides are riddled with the hookworm. We are exceedingly rude to multitudes of our foreign population, and what with our modern efficient methods of banditry, somebody should hold a round-table discussion about us.

But this round-table is about Mexico, so let us get on. Mr. Gamio is a true scientist; I feel he has come nearer to the real life of his own country than either of his compatriots or the liberal minded Mr. Priestley. During his work as director of the Bureau of Anthropology he made a profound sympathetic study of racial origins. His findings presented him with his own special phase of the Mexican problem: that of incorporating this deep-grounded native Indian life with the modern mixed currents of Mexican culture. This incorporation would result in a recognized Indian nation instead of a three-layer, disorganized structure of white, mestizo and Indian. He knows that Mexico and the Indian belong to each other, and consistently refuses to regard him as other than the rightful owner and proprietor of his country. He recognizes the futility of imposing on the Indian customs and standards alien to him: considers the economic and geographical factors and the human one.

The appeal has not all been aimed at the altruistic spirit which may or may not function, according to the weather, in the bosom of man. Each lecturer in turn has pointed out that there would be money, good solid gold to be had out of Mexico in exchange for the same rules of commerce and diplomacy that more important nations are able to enforce from us. They recommend that the wealth now concentrated in the hands of a few vast corporations be loosed and allowed to flow through a thousand new channels, reminding us that there are other riches in Mexico besides oil.

These are books to be read for solid information. The remedies suggested are so very slow the problems they are intended to solve will have died by nature, decayed and reflowered into something else, before they could begin to take effect. Cleaning up is dirty work, this is a mere project for washing face and hands. The thundering racket you hear outside is Mexico getting her pockets picked by her foreign investors.

✍ A Philosopher at Court

New York Herald Tribune Books, August 14, 1927, p. 12.

Review of *A Lady in Waiting to Queen Victoria, Being Some Letters and a Journal of Lady Ponsonby*, edited by her daughter, Magdalen Ponsonby (New York: J. H. Sears and Company, 1927).

In 1853 Miss Mary Elizabeth Bulteel was called to the ceremony of kissing hands on the occasion of her appointment as maid of honor to Queen Victoria. She was then about twenty-two years old, the gifted darling of a family whose vital energy and controversial spirit were famous. Brought up to work gaily at all sorts of serious occupations, she painted and sang and played, studied languages, especially French, read, kept briskly in touch with all political ideas and spent whatever odd moments were left in her home carpenter shop.

Her aunt, Lady Caroline Barrington, was lady-in-waiting and general supervisor of the royal schoolroom nurseries. Her uncle, General Sir Charles Grey, was private secretary to the Queen. Her youth, handsome manners and discreet charm captivated the Queen and she was marked to adorn a court in which, it became gradually apparent, her special qualities of mind were unique. By the time the Queen discovered Miss Bulteel had a mind it was too late. The royal affections had become firmly fixed on her "Dearest Mary" and there they remained for almost half a century.

The new maid of honor began her career at court by rushing away to her room and writing everything to her mother. She did a great deal of letter writing after that and kept a journal besides. The persons who received her letters were happy to answer them in their very best style. She had the kind of mind that incited intelligent response and the kind of temperament that could not endure dullness.

Even Disraeli dared put no less than his best foot forward in her presence. Her collection of personal papers, arranged and edited by her daughter, Magdalen Ponsonby, does nothing to alter our impression of the Victorian court as one of the dullest places of its age: full to bursting of the more cautious virtues, of lush domesticity, of opaque religious habit. But the world hustled on nevertheless; there was plenty of excitement and action; science, philosophy, politics and religious speculation invited the active mind of our heroine, and she was more than equal to them all.

The ladies of the Victorian age have been unfortunate in their legend: it is true that the best of them had decorum to excess, but they never have been sufficiently praised for their vitality. They were so energetic, so robust, so interested in everything. Miss Bulteel had wit to boot; but that was her good luck, and aside from this she was no

accidental manifestation but the natural product of an age overflow-
ing with animal vigor, harnessed to good works by means of moral
conviction. Ceremony irked her all her life, but she knew its value
and observed all its requirements with humorous reservations. Religious doubts assailed her and she explored fearlessly within orthodox
bounds. Her expressed political views were liberal enough to cause
uneasiness among her circle at court but never to the point of scandal. At a time when women's rights women were making the Queen
"so furious she could hardly contain herself" her dearest Mary was
helping to found Girton College for girls and interesting herself in
the working conditions of women, working obliquely to gain those
advantages for her sex which would strengthen them to demand
political rights.

In the mean time her accomplishments as a musician, as an amateur actress were invaluable to the royal home entertainments and
brought her also such friends as [Giovanni] Mario, [Giulia] Grisi,
Fanny Kemble and Ethyl Smith, the composer.

There seems to have been a great deal of very dull dining, much
after dinner singing and playing, and endless carriage drives about
the grounds with the Queen and the fat children behind the four
white ponies. Table tipping caused much excitement of evenings in
the Princess Royal's room, and the Queen was much provoked with
Uncle Charles because, even when he saw the tables tipping, he
refused to believe it. The new maid of honor observed the Prince
Consort, saw that he was good, thoughtful and probably not very
happy. He lacked royal grace, his autocracy was rather that of a tutor,
and his position cut him off from the human contacts that delighted
the Queen.

During the somewhat pointless visitation to France Miss Bulteel
was probably the first of many loyal Britons to note that Victoria's
squat presence outshone the parvenu grandeur of Empress Eugenie.
It was another heart-warming triumph for the good and true over
the beautiful. All the English present noted it. The French opinion is
not recorded. But even so, Miss Bulteel had qualms about the royal
British get-up, and could have wished the lilac cravat, at least, away.

She could not lose her head at any time, and her loyalty was no less loyalty for its keen, smiling eye.

After four years of this sort of thing the most popular maid of honor was ready for an Anglican convent. She had upset her friends by leaning toward the Roman communion, under the influence of Cardinal Newman's works. She asked advice of Lady Canning, wife of the Viceroy of India. With the most charming tact in the world Lady Canning pointed out that religious practices must take account of social appearances, that the impulses of the spirit must be directed for the social good, and that society was apt to be startled and annoyed by any peculiar manifestation of religious fervor. In a word, the spectacle of Miss Bulteel, maid of honor to the Queen, slipping away to be a nun—and so wretchedly young, too!—would create such a sensation that her subsequent usefulness would be seriously impaired. One could only counsel patience and prayer . . . and for fear it might be a Roman convent waiting to swallow the ornament of her times Lady Canning believed that "with all the sad variances and conflicts in our distracted Church we need not (it seems to me) feel impelled to think for an instant of leaving it, as long as the prayer-book is left."

Nothing more is heard of the convent, and two years later Miss Bulteel married Henry Frederick Ponsonby, equerry to the Prince Consort, colonel in the Grenadier Guards, later private secretary to the Queen, and still later Keeper of the Privy Purse. The following year, 1862, she went with her husband to Canada when the Guards were ordered there during a slight threat of trouble with the United States. Lady Ponsonby was a sturdy traveler, and when the Alabama row blew over she came on to the States with her husband. Her bright colloquial style of description seems strangely of to-day, but one paragraph from a letter to her mother describing the opera sounds curiously remote: "Henry had a visit from a Mr. Duncan, to whom we had letters, and he brought us his box at the opera, so off we went after dinner; though I wished very much it had been another night instead. The house is larger than either of the London ones and better lighted, but I thought the music atrocious. It was *Aroldo*—I should say Verdi's very worst—and sung by all the gaps that have failed in London or Paris."

In time the mother of five children, Lady Ponsonby began her education in earnest. She read Rousseau, Tyndall, Huxley, she developed her liberal views, and argued with her husband about the rights of labor. She saw no reason why workingmen should not demand as much wage and leisure as they had the strength to hold out for. In the British control of India she recognized the very triumph of materialism over a "subtle, metaphysical, most highly artistic and developed civilization." John Stuart Mill helped to crystallize many of her social theories, and her growing children caused her to study drawing again, and she founded a drawing society which gave annual exhibitions.

Toward her middle life she met George Eliot, and it is a tribute to the impressive personality of that great dull woman that the independent and spirited Lady Ponsonby approached her with such awe as she had never felt in the presence of any queen, king or emperor: nonetheless she looked about her sharply, and was instantly suspicious of the forced "good talk" that slogged on and on in that distinguished coterie. For years George Eliot influenced her; that genius with a headache could communicate her forlornness, her pessimism, her morality and her abominable literary style to almost any one who came within touching distance.

Under her gayety, high spirits, her tireless interest in everything, Lady Ponsonby must have suffered now and then from psychic headache at least; in her letters to George Eliot she hints for the only time at a mysterious incurable sickness of the soul, for which malady she consults the novelist as one might go to a famous physician. She who had never doubted her capacity in anything suddenly stammers before this ponderous educated and ignorant moralist. For me, this is the most interesting part of this book; it may be fairly easy now to revaluate George Eliot, but there is no explaining the hold she had on the life of her own times; no answer is to be found either in her novels or her letters, or even her personal history. Jack Yeats disposed of her as "an ugly woman who hated handsome men and handsome women" . . . but he was Irish and no Victorian and far away from St. John's Wood, and she is not to be put aside so lightly. Besides the Empress Frederick, whom she outgrew, George Eliot was the only woman to whom Lady Ponsonby gave an equal confidence.

The Queen she loved, and saw clearly. She saw that Disraeli and her other ministers kept the Queen in a state of ignorance as to actual affairs. That she was fickle and vain and more than a little malicious. That she was ambitious to the point of recklessness; that she had an easy kindness of heart for those who pleased her, and something decidedly otherwise for those who did not: not that these things are said anywhere. But all of Lady Ponsonby's affection and loyalty cannot whitewash the unattractive portrait which is built up, incident by petty incident, of the Queen.

As Lady Ponsonby grew older her early world disappeared little by little. She turned to the newer life about her and cultivated the rising generation of writers and politicians. She read Henry James, corresponded with A. C. Benson and Maurice Baring and Edmund Gosse, and began anew her endless speculations on life, literature, philosophy, religion and socialism with her son Arthur, who, having carried royalty's train in his youth, had now gone mildly socialist. His mother had lately been reading Nietzsche, and was tempted to "go back with him to the Egyptian theory of values," when an article of Arthur's was published, and she preferred, with maternal pride, to base her philosophical scheme on his findings.

In May, 1916, at the age of eighty-four, and five months before her death, Lady Ponsonby was still busy comparing ideas and fitting them together into a working scheme, and she almost reached a conclusion: "I like Newman's theory of spiritual development better than the theory I was made to put up with forty years ago—scientific development à la Huxley and Darwin."

✍ Semiramis Was a Good Girl

New York Herald Tribune Books, October 16, 1927, p. 6.

Review of *Memoirs of Catherine the Great of Russia,* trans. Katharine Anthony (New York: Alfred A. Knopf, 1927).

Katharine Anthony is one biographer who manages to make her facts more entertaining than another person's fiction. She sticks to the records, discounting hearsay and word of mouth legend, and patiently gathers the evidence into a brilliant and exciting history that is strong enough to stand by itself.

When her biography of Catherine the Great appeared two years ago I think there was some little disappointment among certain readers who prefer their history spiced with the grotesque. Respectable citizens and properly married householders love to dwell upon the notion of long dead ladies who had 300 lovers.

Catherine the Great was a fine target; she may have murdered her husband and she certainly did seize his throne. She confessed to five or six lovers, and during her reign she employed her energies freely in doing pretty fairly what she pleased. Her legend is, in a left-handed way, a tribute to her powers. But the diaries and letters here published tell even a better story. So disreputable and dangerous were these papers considered that they were circulated privately for many years after her death and finally locked up in the state archives, where they remained until 1907. They were published in Russia in that year and translated into German, properly annotated, by Dr. Erich Boehme. Miss Anthony has followed this text.

Four times, at least, the Empress began her memoirs, each time for a different audience; she tapped her prodigious memory and carefully selected reminiscences poured forth with that seemingly careless profusion which so deceived her contemporary readers. But no matter, she was not able to bring herself further than the death of the Empress Elizabeth. She dwelt on her sad childhood and her terrible eighteen years at the Russian Court while Elizabeth ruled. Over and over she began, but there was a barrier over which she could not set foot, and we have only the briefest notes on all that took place after the strange death of Peter, her husband.

Her childhood memories remained acute, and even in middle age she wrote vividly of the fat aunt who slept with sixteen evil-smelling pug dogs in a small room; and of the other gentle maimed aunt, who loved only maimed creatures and collected wounded birds. Her first governess, she says, taught her to be devious and politic. Her second, Babet Cardel, regulated little Fike's character, and no nonsense about it. She was born an obscure German princess, with a lucky relationship to the Empress of Russia, but had she minded the moral axioms stuffed into her tender ears by her pastor she might never have become Empress of all the Russias herself.

When Empress Elizabeth of Russia wished to marry off her half-witted heir to the throne, Peter, she sent for the fifteen-year-old Princess Friedrike of Zerbst and the marriage was accomplished, after a fashion. The Princess changed her name and her religion and had a dangerous illness; got her first glimpse of the illiterate, semi-barbarian court in which she was to live and learned a little to defend herself, all before the ceremony. Afterward, for nine years, she lived a virgin with her husband and finally took Sergei Saltikov for a lover, in order to have an heir to the throne.

She tells this astounding story quite simply, with many details, by the way. She wrote as one having literary ambitions and would not spare any pains to get her brilliant effects. Voltaire was her master; she had a Gallic passion for lightness of touch, for irony and wit: she could not endure dullness, she vowed; yet we have her word for it that she was bored for her first eighteen years at the Russian court.

On her accession to the throne she changed all that. The rest of her life was devoted to empire making, to the furthering of her private ambitions, to the improving of her mind and to living at constant high pressure. These memoirs are not from the pen of a Semiramis; Catherine the Great had, or fancied she had, a substratum of all the domestic virtues. To her last day she believed that to be a good wife she had needed only to find a good husband. She was, as Miss Anthony has noted, a good actress, as an empress should be; and even here, in these memoirs, stripped of erotic Byzantine gold leaf of fable, she remains one of the most remarkable and interesting women in history.

The translation is done beautifully in Miss Anthony's rich and forceful prose.

✍ Misplaced Emphasis

New York Herald Tribune Books, June 3, 1928, p. 7.

Review of *We Are Incredible,* by Margery Latimer
(New York: J. H. Sears and Company, 1928).

For the last three or four years Miss Margery Latimer has been mentioned with increasing praise as one of the younger writers whose career would be worth watching. She belongs definitely to that group whose method and point of view contain what certain contemporary critics define as "the element of to-dayness."

I don't know what this means, but I, too, recognize a tendency when I see it, though I should be at a loss to describe it in anything like so neat a phrase. Miss Latimer has written some noticeable short stories, exhibiting technical sureness and certain arbitrary but effective slant on human character. She has worked honestly, and has not neglected to sharpen and polish the tools of her craft. This is the mark of a good guildsman in any age, and I should never think of calling it modern.

The element of to-dayness must be looked for in other phases of Miss Latimer's work. It may lie in a certain tendency to empiricism in her psychological treatment of human nature, or in her personal conception of her rights over the characters which, after all, she created herself, or possibly it lies in her own attitude toward life and the vocation of authorship. Young authors, flushed with the lively work of reducing all life to scientific terms, forget to wait on the findings of science before rushing in with their own theories. Still, as scientific experimenters they are creative but no longer gods. So they assume a homely posture in the presence of their creatures, and quarrel with them, or praise them, as if they were rather difficult neighbors, or friends whom they feel bound to placate on grounds of personal affection.

Miss Latimer does both. She gropes at the clews to personality in her characters as if they were strangers to her, and she is learning about them herself while she exposes them to you. She stands on even ground with them, and bears a personal animus toward them as if she were defending herself against them. She mingles heartily in their affairs, pursues with venom the ones she hates, and is marvelously romantic and short sighted about the ones she likes. To my mind, the reasons for liking Dora and Mitchell and hating Myrtle, Rex and the children and despising poor Joe Teeter, who is quite as admirable as any one else in the book, remain a mystery that justifies the otherwise quite irrelevant title: *We Are Incredible.*

Two persons die in this book, due to the malign influence of Hester Linden's New Thoughtism. Another has been fished out of the canal on the same account, some years before the story opens.

This is the tragedy then: the story of pauper spirits and confusion of values. Miss Latimer pursues her victims to the bitter end, exposing the shabby seams of their souls without pity, but with some irony and an accumulation of wounding detail. No accent or inflection is spared of the wretched girl Dora, who is a snob and cannot see any beauty in common life, but wishes to escape into the rarefied atmosphere of Hester, where there are servants and literary conversations—of an appalling kind—and thus avoid marrying a youth who owns a dairy and answers to the name of Joe Teeter. These are his only crimes, but she does not pardon them. Hester has taught her better.

Dora is sister to the tactless Myrtle and unawakened would have grown into a diluted version of the older woman. But she is corrupted by a glimpse of luxury and easy living and mistakes Hester Linden's somewhat unfortunate mannerisms for the outward and visible signs of an inner and spiritual grace. Hester apes the lesser prophets in deforming her disciples for the sake of shining by contrast; she exercises her love of power by destroying purblind souls. She can find no others evidently.

The prime victims, Dora and Mitchell, struggle against her influence in the growth of their love, and Dora at least has blood in her, so that she seems a fine furry animal it is a pity to entrap. The man is irritating, but we have met him before in young American fiction and we will meet him again, so a word or two is necessary. He is terrified and cannot come to grips with reality; he slinks and lies to himself and when he bursts out with the truth it is inspired not by a clear view of his own futilities, but by hatred of the person he fancies to be the cause of them. He lacks vitality and wit for even one complete way of life, so his mind swings aimless between half-formulated philosophies: and he divides his love between two women because he is not sufficient for one. He is a lazy, would-be artist, and he believes his muddled mind and physical disgusts are the marks of a rare temperament. There are too many young men like this in our contemporary fiction, but they, too, have an element of to-dayness. Miss Latimer has selected a particularly ripe specimen and she exposes him with a fine slashing female realism.

Well, the two defeated and unsatisfied lovers meet death under a bush in Hester Linden's well clipped garden, and that is no sort of repartee, because Hester receives it as a personal tribute to her power and essential rightness, and the story ends, for her, on a hopeful note. She feels mystically renewed—for she is past fifty—because she can now possess them both in her mind, forever young, beautiful and deathless.

Miss Latimer pushes through to her climax with a great deal of energy and leads the reader to expect one annihilating blow aimed at Hester. Suddenly she seems to lose heart for hatred, she relents and lets her off. This is a pity, but then the deus ex machina always gets away in triumph: it is an old Greek convention. The trouble is this is no goddess, but an exceptionally silly woman talking and behaving in a highfaluting manner, and in the logic of events she should have been found out. It is sad to die for such tawdry dreams as Dora's and Mitchell's—I don't believe they would have done it.

This is an impressive study of the effects a glimpse of culture— even the near-variety—may have on the uninformed minds of the young in a small American town; a well planned, well executed drama of a girl who died, when all is said, because the sight of a fine white linen monogrammed handkerchief in the hands of her lover made her hands and feet feel too large. Can this misplaced emphasis be symptoms of some dangerous disease eating at the vitals of young Americans? I greatly fear it is.

✍ Hand-Book of Magic

New Republic, vol. 55, no. 712 (July 25, 1928), p. 257.

Review of *A Mirror for Witches*, by Esther Forbes
(Boston: Houghton Mifflin Company, 1928).

Miss Esther Forbes was born in Worcester, Massachusetts, where historical societies flourish in the shade of a great library and museum of New England antiquities. But it requires more than mere devoted plundering of the mildewed rubbish heap of history to write such a book as this. I think Miss Forbes, like her own Doll Bilby, has evoked her pre-conscious memories of old Massachusetts, and breathed out again upon the pages the legends she breathed in with the air of her childhood.

She has held up not only a mirror for witches, but a magic reflection of New England's past. Even her style, a highly artificial affair that could be disastrous in less capable hands, is quite convincing. It might well be the result of saturation in old documents, letter books and diaries, or a slightly diminished echo of the old English rhythms of speech which yet survive in rural New England. I don't know if the soundness and movingness of her total effect depend on this style: I know it gives an almost perfect illusion, and carries the story without effort. Now and again Miss Forbes lapses into deliberate and charming pastiche, as if to say: "Remember, this is not really a pious seventeenth-century gaffer turning over once more an uneasy memory"—but these asides are few, and the whole thing has an air of rightness.

At times the narrative reads like a transcript from the witch tales that conscientious country preachers wrote down for Increase Mather's famous collection. The history of the Thumb twins is along a classic pattern, and the trial scene is a magnificent re-creation of the melancholy scenes at Salem in 1692. Miss Forbes has set her tragedy somewhat earlier, in order to give her witch the stellar role. But Doll Bilby takes her place in that dark group of women who died in the Terror, herself as real as if her name and history appeared in the records. The true interest lies in Miss Forbes' understanding of the witch state of mind in a highly imaginative, morbidly emotional young girl.

Doll Bilby is the adopted daughter of a New England sea captain. Her mother had been burned for a witch in Brittany, and even in Doll's childhood she is feared and hated for a witch. In her loneliness she confuses the stories her mother told her with actual events, she cannot discern between dream and reality, either in the past or present. She ends by believing herself compacted to the Devil, and mistakes a mysterious mortal lover for an even more mysterious fiend. As her hallucinations grow and her actions become more strange, the evidence against her is, to the New England mind of her day, overwhelming. Her death in prison cheats the gallows.

This is the simple plot, but told with such candid warmth, so much sly wit and detached irony, such a lively march of episode, that it makes a superbly entertaining novel.

✍ Marc Lescarbot

New Republic, vol. 56, no. 716 (August 22, 1928), pp. 24–25.

Review of *Nova Francia: A Description of Acadia, 1606*, trans. P. Erondelle, 1609 (New York: Harper and Brothers, 1928).

Marc Lescarbot was a Frenchman, a wit, something of a poet, and a scholar devoted to the homely wisdom of Montaigne. He was a barrister also: and his philosophy did not save him from a temporary embitterment when he suffered an injustice in the Paris courts. When his chief client, Jean de Biencourt, Seigneur de Poutrincourt, invited him on a voyage to visit the French territories in America, he accepted and spent the year 1606–7 in Port Royal. His description of Acadia was published in 1609, and immediately translated into English.

Lescarbot had the delightfully excursive and literary mind of his time, a correct code of morals, and a civilized heart. Everything he saw on his travels reminded him of something he had read, which in turn reminded him of something else he had read, and so he made a trip around the world, and back into ancient times, by way of history, mythology and poetry, arriving at Acadia and the Indian customs by a thousand roads. He looked about him, and set down a substantial account of what he saw: then searched his prodigious memory for contrast and comparison among the Gauls and the Picts, the ancient Hebrews, the Persians, the Egyptians, the Romans and even the modern French.

As a poet, he delighted in the strange ceremonies, the form and beauty of savage life. As a moralist, he condemned in them only the vices he condemned in all men and praised them for whatever virtues are the common property of good souls. As a Roman Catholic, he wished to bring the poor savage into the ample fold of the true Faith: and as a practical man and a loyal Frenchman he could not help seeing that his distinguished friend Poutrincourt was doing a great work in helping to build up a stout French government in this territory that lay dangerously adjacent to lands already claimed by the English and the Dutch.

Today his book is valuable for permanent things: for style, for historical truth, for charming wit and leisurely learning. When it was first published, Richard Hakluyt observed that it was not only a fascinating travel book, but an excellent political argument. At his request, Pierre Erondelle, a Huguenot—possibly a refugee—then living in London, translated that part of the book here reprinted, and dedicated it to the Bright Star of the North, Prince Henry of Britain.

Erondelle called the Prince's attention to the fact that Lescarbot had dedicated his book to a King, two Queens and the Dauphin: politically, this had a sinister significance, and the translator urged upon His Highness the need for immediate activity in colonizing Virginia. Plainly, the French were at work in Acadia, and the settling of the adjacent territories for England must proceed without delay, or those rich resources would go to waste, England would continue to be pestered overmuch by people living in misery, and, above all, the poor savages would be exposed to the dangers of a false religion.

The charming and adroit book of M. Lescarbot was translated and published at once, therefore, not so much as good reading matter, but as a warning to the English that Virginia was too sparsely settled and too near the thriving French posts for English comfort. Their enjoyment of M. Lescarbot's urbane style must have been marred considerably by the dire propaganda they could discern between the lines.

The fashionable anxiety, of French and English alike, to carry the gospel to the American savages, had the wholesome effect of stimulating emigration from both countries. Lescarbot addressed a benevolent message to the future generations of Indians. They would all be happily civilized in time, and he hoped they would read his book and "bless them that have employed themselves in their conversion, and reformation of their incivility."

✍ The Family

New York Herald Tribune Books, October 7, 1928, p. 2.

Review of *Nothing Is Sacred*, by Josephine Herbst
(New York: Coward-McCann, 1928).

You need never have lived in Miss Herbst's world to know that it is inhabited by human beings and not manikins outfitted with mouthpieces to spout the philosophy and the personal grievances of the author. Hundreds of young American novelists, those who have publishers and those who are hunting publishers, have milled around in the great American scene; trying to explain, discredit or justify it as though it were merely a specially painted back-drop for their own frustrated personal dramas. For the most part they expose merely another wounded soul who couldn't bear his family or the stupid neighbors and who suffered when he remembered his first bungling attempts at love.

This is the story of an American family in a modest way of life, each member of the group filled with a perfectly legitimate desire for happiness and success in living. The author introduces this family at a crisis threatening grave danger and deep humiliation, owing to the stupid conduct of a son-in-law. It is a matter of money, and though kindness to a brother in distress is "part of the ritual, really," still the members of Harry Norland's lodge are rather disposed to make a moral example of him. The old mother, Mrs. Winters, takes on herself the burden of saving him, not for his sake, for she despises him, but for the honor of the family.

There is a kind of bitter comedy in the episodes that follow, but you will not feel like laughing. You will not find a trace of sentimental revolt or sentimental hatred or special pleading. These are human beings, born in a certain set of circumstances to a certain mode of existence, but the individual creature shows clearly through the pattern behavior of the group. The men carry Eversharp pencils and drive Fords if they can't do better—though they all hope to do better— and are ambitious to get to the top in local society and business circles. The embezzling son-in-law tries to restore his self-approval by making a great advertising campaign for Fintella, the joyfood of the nation. Forty-year-old Hazel dances with her nineteen-year-old nephew in the Orange Blossom cabaret and feels she is seeing life. Julia experiments with marital infidelity and it sours on her frightfully. Hilda wants love and gets it by sheer force. But all these things are secondary beside the acute, sudden glimpses of inner character, revealed by means of petty gestures and phrases on the part of the persons themselves. Each has separateness and his incommunicable fate.

The old mother is superb. The story of her life, struggles and death is told with touching gravity and tenderness. I know only one other old woman in a novel who compares with her for pure reality—Mrs. Moore in *A Passage to India*. This mother is the core of the family, and the efforts of the daughters to destroy all the accumulated rubbish in her attic after her death is only one more effort to break the terrible bonds of blood from which each one is blindly struggling to escape. It is no good; the family still exists, the bond has nothing to do with things. They might burn the house over their heads and still they are bound.

The passion and interest and energy of this novel proceed from the concentrated forces of the author; the life does not depend on the material. It is a short book, the sentences are short, the words are simple, and still the prose has poetic grace and style. It is not angular, spare, stark, dry or any of the more kindly synonyms for jerky dullness. It is beautiful and full with the fullness of a perfect economy and final choice of phrase. It is all in one piece from beginning to end, and must be read line by line, or you will miss something important to the story.

There are no chapters, but merely a double paragraph now and then to indicate a pause or a shift of scene. It has been done before, precisely as the American family has been done. But Miss Herbst has made them both her own by doing them naturally and perfectly.

✍ The Hundredth Role

New York Herald Tribune Books, October 7, 1928, p. 16.

Review of *The Book of Catherine Wells*, with introduction by her husband, H. G. Wells (Garden City, N.Y.: Doubleday, Doran and Company, 1928).

Probably the best that a married pair have to offer each other at the end of a long life together is a courteous mutual apology. But this should be privately spoken and the secret guarded. Husbands and wives do ill to explain each other in print, more especially if the one explained is dead.

The preface written by Mr. H. G. Wells for the collected short stories of his wife is a singularly unfortunate example of the literature of marital bereavement. Catherine Wells was a noble wife, a happy mother and the maker of a free, kind and hospitable home. She was sweet and valiant, faithful, wise and self-forgetful. Pity and habitual helpfulness were very characteristic of her. She was stoical in suffering, shy and reserved in her real emotions and briskly impatient of nonsense in any form. She died with courage and dignity after months of suffering.

All this, it seems to me, should have served fully for the enrich-

ment of Mr. Wells's life while she lived and for the present consolation of his memories. It is rather sadly beside the point in a preface
written with the stated purpose of introducing Catherine Wells, not
as the wife of her distinguished husband but as a talented writer of
short stories.

The literary judgment of Mr. Wells seems somewhat at fault, too,
as well as his taste in other matters. The short stories in this book
of Catherine Wells have qualities of delicacy, tender feeling and a restrained fancy, but the book as a whole belongs to her husband and
will attract the reader because his name is conspicuous on the cover.

This is sad and the end of a story full of irony. Amy Catherine Rob-
bins meant to become a biologist; she married H. G. Wells while she
was a member of his class in practical biology. This was about 1893.
They had £50 between them and small expectations of a long life, for
neither of them was in good health. Mrs. Wells developed at once the
hundred-sided capacity necessary for successful wifehood to a driving, ambitious, vastly confused but completely self-centered literary
man. The compromises, the adjustments of temperament to the common life were mainly hers: she furnished the faith and the attention
to practical details of daily life; she was the charming companion and
the good housekeeper; she acted as private secretary, literary agent
and shock-absorber for her busy husband, and she had the legitimate
satisfaction of seeing him famous and wealthy at an early age. The
role of hostess to the many friends of fame now devolved upon her.
She became a talented amateur actress and the inventive entertainer
of her two children. Her gardens were works of art. Her husband and
his friends even took the liberty of changing her name to fit their
conception of her domestic character. They called her Jane and she
answered to it cheerfully.

In the classic role of woman her life was complete. Yet this indefati-
gable woman asked for one thing more. She asked for one fragment of
her mind that might be her own to use as she liked. She resolutely set
herself to write and took no one, not even her husband, into her confidence. Through agencies unconnected with her husband and under
her right name of Catherine she attempted to market her stories, re-

jecting the easy use of her husband's influence. Most of the stories remained unpublished.

Jane had quite supplanted Catherine. When Mrs. Wells searched that part of her mind left for her own uses there remained only the heroically suppressed preoccupations with death, the terror fantasies of ghosts, of childish disappointments and griefs, the young maiden dreams of frustrated romantic love. All the adult experiences of her life since marriage refused to be transmuted into literature. She could not evoke the realities of Jane on paper.

Within less than a year after her death the stories she could not publish by herself have been collected, chosen by her husband as final critic and introduced with his praise, his name joined to hers on the cover. Death served to force her withheld confidences and shatter her last reserves. The stories offer a strange contrast to the portrait her husband gives of a vivid, tireless, beautiful woman whose endless good sense and ground loyalty to the man of her choice make her a model for all good women and prove that she was a writer of very slender talents. An act of conscious cruelty could never have been so subtle.

"She stuck to me so sturdily that in the end I stuck to myself," says Mr. H. G. Wells. That is her epitaph.

✍ The Dark Ages of New England

New York Evening Post, November 3, 1928, p. 8.

Review of *Cotton Mather, Keeper of the Puritan Conscience*, by Ralph and Louise Boas (New York: Harper, 1928).

The history of Cotton Mather is also a history of New England from 1633 until 1728; his life must always be considered with reference to his grandfathers, John Mather and Richard Mather; his father, Increase Mather, and the whole petty, turbulent and essentially ugly political history of that period in the Massachusetts Bay colony.

Ralph and Louise Boas have selected and arranged this bewildering

mass of polemic, misstatement, special pleading and naïve confessions which is documentary evidence that the early Puritans are not
mere nightmare-fantasies; and out of it they have brought Cotton
Mather, quite alive and much more incredible than his legend has
made him appear.

So far as is humanly possible, I do believe, the authors have spared
this hapless man. They wished to be scrupulously fair to him, and
they have been. Scrupulous fairness in biographers seems to mean a
gentle leaning toward the side of their hero, a careful building up of
the better elements of his defense. They have used incidents selected
for color, for drama, for sketching in the background, and have quoted
liberally from the rude old chronicles; the result is a very fine biography of Cotton Mather, and another book as long as this one might
be written with the things they have left out.

There were no poets, no philosophers, no artists, no singers in the
Massachusetts Bay colony. There were no military geniuses and never
a Governor whose stature exceeded that of a petty tyrannical politician. There was no first-rate theologian after John Cotton, and he
was their only courtier until his son-in-law Increase Mather proved
himself one during the Charter crisis.

In short, all the elements of civilization were lacking in that life
and the religious practices were as little humane as, and considerably less imaginative than, those of the early Aztecs. The theocrats
had political cunning and interpreted the terms of their Charter with
such fraudulent and pious logic they managed to deceive the Kings of
England and function under a system that was illegal, if not treasonable, for nearly sixty years. But they thought handsomely of themselves and documented themselves with that peculiar shamelessness
that belongs to the self-righteous in any land, in any time.

The record lacks dignity. Rule and rigor enough: bloodshed terror enough: a tremendous booming of phrase: a hard, blind straining
toward grandeur of feeling and concept: a fair imitation at times of the
spirit of man in travail: but the basic quality of dignity that rests on
fineness of imagination was lacking utterly. Calvin had bequeathed
to them a great idea, but they could not grasp it. Probably never before

in the history of religion had man's idea of God, the relation of man to God and to man, fallen so far below what is humanly permissible, as it did in the great theocratic state, the new Israel founded by a dozen preachers and two dozen upper middle-class British merchants in Massachusetts Bay.

This accounts for the significance of Cotton Mather. He was of the third generation from the two most distinguished men in the colony. He was their fine flower, the ultimate seed of their culture. He had their snobbish respect for the printed word and their inability to learn. He combined perfectly their hardness of heart, their opinionist logic, and their shoddy mysticism. He was a master of befuddling oratory and wore them down by the sheer volume of his words. He practiced their politics against them for his own ends, and they were long in waking up to this fact. In his blindness he failed to grasp the gradual emergence of the popular mind from medieval faith into what was known as rationalism: this marked the final triumph of that ambitious, slowly rising middle class that had made the reformatory possible. So he survives. He is by no means dead.

The authors have had access to a vast bibliography on this subject. They have preferred to abide by one or two classical legends that John Cotton and not Nathanial Ward was the author of the "Body of Liberties," that bloodthirsty code of the early colony, and that Cotton Mather was the shadow and the echo of his distinguished father all his life. They have omitted his battle for control of the press in Boston through his brother-in-law, Bartholomew Green, and have stressed the fact that he did not attend the witch trials, omitting the more important fact that he did attend the preliminary hearings, where the fate of the accused wretch was settled before ever he saw the courtroom. His fondness for writing damaging anonymous letters has been touched upon lightly. In every way this portrait is sympathetically softened wherever possible; Cotton Mather has never lacked for apologists, and he still has friends at court after two hundred years. There is too much of him left in our world, even yet. To condemn him utterly is to condemn ourselves.

✍ The Virgin and the Unicorn

New York Herald Tribune Books, February 17, 1929, pp. 1–2.

Review of *The True Heart*, by Sylvia Townsend Warner
(New York: Viking Press, 1929).

First a cautionary word: This novel is not whimsical. It is not fantastic. Unless I am mistaken in the intention of the author, it might be called fantasy, in the sense of being a deliberate effort to separate the reader for a moment from his ordinary mood of objectivity and set him down in a world of symbolic truths.

Having knocked at least two crutch words from under me, I must now stand on my feet and discuss this book calmly. It seems to me that *The True Heart* is Miss Warner's personal contribution to a venerable tradition of English feeling. Every thing in it is peculiarly English: the filial love of the sovereign, the tender admiration for the aristocracy, the warm appreciation for the virtues of the lower classes, the love of nature, the beautiful writing that smooths and sharpens and pats and points and models the images into correct, somewhat formalized outlines.

As for Sukey Bond: She is hallowed by time also, and 10,000 faithful, courageous, suffering but triumphant English virgins might step forth from the covers of books and bid her welcome. We have still another variation of the lovely myth of the virgin and the unicorn; of Una and the Lion; of white hot ploughshares withholding their rage from the feet of a chaste woman. Sukey loves the unicorn, he bows his head to her knee, he kisses her with wild, sly lips; he flees; he is gone, and she goes through terrible painful adventures to find him again. Her dangers are many, from tramps on the road and from the keeper of a brothel, but to these her virgin state is still sacred: all good Christians know that not even the wild beasts would offer a scratch to an innocent maid seeking her love.

Sukey remains a symbol, a figure of legend. Into her Miss Warner has poured her own rather wistful, touching, somewhat tragic interpretation of this old legend of the maiden, love and fate. The imbecile lad, Eric (the unicorn!), is no more than a puff of thistledown caught between the fingers of a day-dreaming girl. Indeed, the whole book, in spite of a few living characters, a few credibly breathing animals, a few strong words, real hay, real mud, real sky and tree and moon lovingly described, is like the changing landscape of a dream where figures move on some ageless errand.

One point is interesting: the episodes and conversation are the stuff of dreams, but the inner moods of these hallucinary persons seem at times almost real. The sharp division between the actual event and the repercussion of the event on their imaginations gives the impression of a drama of reality being played in a closed house, while strangers knock noisily at the door shouting an irrelevant message.

There is a great deal of quick, graceful writing in this book: good phrases: "I fell in love as though I were falling asleep." Acute humor: the rector, disgruntled after years of marriage to an ambitious, beautiful, unloving wife, suddenly decides that, since she cares nothing for him, there is no reason why he should be on time for luncheon. Some psychological touches seem right and true: Sukey, sitting alone in the snow, in a field, homeless, friendless, hungry, separated from her love, begins to weep. After the manner of dreaming minds, she substitutes a generalized human sorrow for her present sharp grief, and transfers her own sufferings to an imagined, perhaps even an invented, suffering. She weeps in bitter affliction for the cruelty of men towards wolves.

The theme is on the grand scale of legend: Youth with its blind searching eyes walks in a waking dream of faith through adventures that would require, for a conscious mind, a desperate courage. After tremendous perils, the end is gained and the eyes are opened in amazement that so much pain had been required to gain so simple and homely a thing.

Yet Sukey's inventory at the end, when in childbirth she remembers clearly for the last time the precise magic of her young illusion, is flawed by a lyrical tenseness straining the situation beyond its capacity: there remain, however, two symbolic figures still gesticulating in a dream: Sukey the servant, humble, suffering, patient, the perpetually faithful, the blindly loving woman; Eric the illuminated, unconscious, irresponsible, evasive man, loving and forgetful by turns.

I don't know if this is what Miss Warner had in mind. It is what occurs to me as I read.

✍ Not So Lost!

New York Herald Tribune Books, March 3, 1929, p. 4.

Review of *The Lost Art. Letters of Seven Famous Women*,
ed. Dorothy Van Doren (New York: Coward-McCann, 1929).

Discretion recommends that letters be put away in a safe place until both sender and receiver are quietly dead with their generation. It would be exciting to be alive fifty years from now when our contemporary letters—some of them marked urgently, "Burn this!"—are brought out and published. Think of all the gayety, the brilliance, the passion, the political information, the tragic adventures of our days recorded minutely and now lying about in chests, in trunks and strong boxes! I don't believe it is a lost art. Women are still writing letters. It is their notorious indiscretion, their frankness, their beautiful interest in daily living, their humorous disregard of consequences of the written word that give charm to the letters of women and cause the letters of long dead women to be so touching and so alive.

For these seven women letter writing was a subsidiary art, one of the hundred ramifications of the vast female duty to please. They might therefore practice it without restraint. These seven were not professional pleasers. Indeed, without exception they refused to be pleasing except where they chose. Yet each had at least one dearly loved human creature to whom she addressed herself with her defenses laid aside, and the result is, quite accidentally, good literature. However idly or hastily these women wrote, under whatever conditions, they possess in common a developed style, point, an openness of heart and a desire to share themselves, to disclose their moods and thoughts; in short, honestly to communicate with the person addressed.

These women, whose lives cover from the birth of the first to the death of the last more than two centuries in time, have been selected carefully by the editor for the wide divergences of their worldly conditions, the diverse qualities of their minds and the great range of their emotions. Lady Mary Wortley Montagu, Mary Wollstonecraft, Abigail Adams, Charlotte Brontë, Jane Welsh Carlyle, Jane Austen and Margaret Fuller in one group surely merit at least the word representative. I have read all the published letters of all these women, and I appreciate Mrs. Van Doren's intensive selection: by choosing sharply a very small number of letters she has managed to plot each life clearly over a long stretch of time. It is important to note the changeless character of these women. They were quite integral and sound from first to last. The changes occurring in them were merely the logical developments of fixed character reacting steadily to events and external forces. Of them all, Lady Mary Wortley Montagu is for me the most humanly attractive. But that may be because I love the gallant, talkative, rationalistic, inquisitive, abundant eighteenth century, and Lady Mary was nobly a child of her time. Above all, she had a certain grandeur in the face of reverses of fortune that the others lacked. In the end, they all had some mystical consolation, some refuge. Without religion, without love of husband or child (for her adored daughter, Lady Bute, was almost as famously indifferent as the cold-hearted child of Mme. de Sevigné), without any resources or beliefs above this world, Lady Mary was, quite simply, unlicked to the last. She cast in her lot with reason and stood firm. When the props of reason fell, she did not fly weeping to belated spiritual reinforcements, for there was no vulgarity in her healthy nature. She believed her daughter had married a fool, she intimated it too clearly, but saw no reason why this should affect the relationship between mother and daughter. When after many years of separation from her husband she had occasion to write to him, the reasons that had seemed good for leaving him held good for her staying away. Her son had disclosed

himself to her as a rake and a species of imbecile, and mother-love did
nothing to cloud her fixed view of him in this twin rôle. She was all
for going ahead under full sail, and she kept herself at least a knot in
advance of her thriving times. She was on terms of armed truce with
all the wits and politicians of her day, and was even hardy enough
to exchange lampoons with Pope, an encounter in which she sustained a not unqualified defeat: he could beat anybody at the rhymed
vituperative couplet, but Lady Mary commanded a viperish prose.
A really tremendous spirit, full of wit and courage and fire and the
divine salt of humor: I hope Mrs. Van Doren's selections will send
large numbers of readers direct to a volume of Lady Mary's letters.

Mary Wollstonecraft must have found her world a singularly dreadful one: she was a woman cursed with deep emotions, a quick argumentative mind, a frustrated religious conscience, and a rigid set of
moral scruples. She had picked up the pedantic social theories which
heralded the nineteenth century, and J. J. Rousseau's sentimental
humanistic libertarianism now bore fruit in some horrid schemes to
right all social wrong. Her radical feminism seemed monstrous to
her times. Her delicate high beauty did not save her from a life of
hardships incident to the disaster of having been born with an in-
quiring mind. She was thirty-five years old before she had a lover,
and then a basely inferior one. She bore her child out of wedlock and
was deserted. The letters in this collection are all addressed to her
American lover, Gilbert Imlay. They show her at her weakest. She is
simply a terrified creature trying to beat her way through a jungle of
conflicting thoughts and feelings. She stuck to her principles and her
pride, and lived three years longer, to be the wife of William Godwin,
a pedant and a charlatan, and the mother of Mary Shelley. Her *Vindi-
cation of the Rights of Women* remains a monument to her boldness,
her anger, her generosity, and her frustration. Her luck was the worst
of them all.

Abigail Adams was the tranquil wife of one President of the United
States and the mother of another. Even she, in her demure, snug-
bosomed way, was a woman of spirit. She was a superb friend to her
husband, indeed, she was the only one of the seven who had an end-

less benevolence toward her man. True, she had the best husband of them all. But she might have created the husband side of him whole out of her large wisdom. Hers was the right degree of wifely blindness, of womanly tolerance, of faith. She made a serious career of wifehood, and her success was complete.

Charlotte Brontë's letters were of a piece with her books: grave, sententious, emotional, with fine stretches of rhetoric and sudden homely passages of feminine mother-wit. She was afraid of love and a trifle bitter about men, after her experiences with her father, her brother and the country curates whom she ridiculed savagely. She married one of these curates after an eight-year siege, and in spite of her modest efforts to breathe forth the proper aura of bridal joy, it is impossible not to feel that she carried her mental reservations about love and marriage from a chilly bed to a cold grave. She disapproved of Miss Jane Austen on the score of that lady's too persistent irony and lack of heart; while judging from her gossipy, deliciously self-possessed letters, Miss Austen would not have thought of Charlotte Brontë at all.

Jane Welsh Carlyle had mental reservations about everybody except her husband. She was spiteful and gossipy and affectionate and warmhearted. She loved her genius, admired him, tormented him, suffered and cried to him for help, petted and spoiled and rebuked him grievously for forty exciting years. I think the Carlyles got more out of their marriage than other couples far more celebrated for domestic happiness. It never staled on them. Carlyle called her his "little long-suffering fellow-pilgrim." That deserves to stand beside John Cotton's address to his Sarah: "Dear wife and comfortable yoke-fellow!" Margaret Fuller, Bostonian transcendentalist, journalist and the most famous blue-stocking of her day, went to Italy out of enthusiasm for Mazzini's revolution, and stayed to marry Count d'Ossoli for his handsome eyes. She boasted of his ignorance of books, and wrote tender defenses of him to her family.

In these letters the women who wrote them manage to capture their own essences; it makes an impressive showing of grand human qualities. They deserve to be remembered, to be praised.

✍ Moral Waxworks Exposed

New York Herald Tribune Books, May 12, 1929, p. 4.

Review of *The Devil Is a Woman*, poems by Alice Mary Kimball
(New York: Alfred A. Knopf, 1929).

When I heard Mrs. Kimball read some of these poems in manu-
script, a year or two ago, they impressed me first for their outrageous
humor and witty, rather merciless slant on the opaque, unteachable
human mind as it exists in American rural communities. But this is
by no means all. Reading them again, I have been ushered through
a museum of spiritual horrors, where pietist dogma is disclosed in
the various shapes of meanness and noble theories of conduct have
incarnated themselves stiffened into the postures of fanaticism.

   Mrs. Kimball has left out the neighborly barn burnings and the
classic ax murders of New England, but these are about all, and they
are implicit in the background. She has told these horrifying stories
with a curiously detached, broadly comic attitude, thus rightly rob-
bing them of the spirit of tragedy: and her method is precisely adapted
to get the effect she wanted. Rhymed verse would not have done,
and it is hard to imagine these narratives in prose: Mrs. Kimball has
adopted an oddly halting rhythmic prose with an occasional rhyme
popped neatly into its right place; and her attack on morals and manners is as savage, speedy and venomed with ridicule as the work of
an eighteenth century pamphleteer. She writes in a heavy vernacu-
lar usually as unwieldy as a hay cart: and her phrases coast along as
surely as Kate McQuigg's Ford, on its errands through Dorset as a
perambulating beauty shop. Kate McQuigg tells some of the tales:
among them "The Mating Flight of Stasia Whitsett," an epic yarn of
the lengths to which a New England virgin of good family went to
justify herself for marrying an Italian farmer. The title piece, "The
Devil Is a Woman," is the outrageously funny history of a contemporary St. Anthony. "Mrs. Doane Comes Back" is a touching story
of mere physical weariness, and "The Lord's Child" sums up Elmer

Gantry in a mere three or four pages. Human malice, dullness, self-righteous blindness, petty vanity and ambitions: it takes a species of genius to make a good work out of such materials, and Mrs. Kimball has quite certainly done it. In spite of staking out her territory so sharply, giving a local flavor to the crimes committed by good and bad alike, describing so accurately preferences in food and dress and architecture, she somehow succeeds in reminding you that these tales are universal, they belong to the folk-myth of all countries, they seem unreal only because much of human conduct is incredible; varying only in surface detail, they are the product of life lived at a certain level of darkness in any part of the world.

✍ Old Gods and New Messiahs

New York Herald Tribune Books, September 29, 1929, pp. 1–2.

Review of *Idols Behind Altars*, by Anita Brenner (New York: Payson and Clarke, 1929).

This book is like an ancient chronicle, owing its existence to so many sources, so many articulate lives, that the author does not even attempt the impossible task of acknowledging all her indebtedness. The anthropologist, the explorer, the teacher, the artist, the folk-heroes, the makers of the legend and miracle have joined in pouring out their riches to make of this a communal work, like everything else that comes out of Mexico. It is true there are a few names to lend reality, and the attempt to present reality is a brave one, but there is a portentous air of legend in the style, and in spite of herself the author writes in a heightened mood of one enchanted and convinced by a miracle. Mexico is a disturbing country, and it has this effect on those who love it. The contradictions are too violent in this land of miracles, of Messiahs, of venal politicians, of dedicated scholars, of sober artists and extravagant dreams.

Miss Brenner wrote her book, the first attempt at an ordered story of art and artists in Mexico, with the official sanction and the un-

limited aid of the University of Mexico. She has the equipment of a
good annalist: youth and enthusiastic sympathies, the gift of close
and penetrating observation, a genius for listening and remembering
what she hears and an admirably energetic style. She was accompanied on her search by Tina Modotti and Edward Weston, whose
photographs are more than mere illustrations: and her material has
the freshness of things gathered by word of mouth and through the
eye, for later Mexican history has never been written fully and survives in stories told and songs sung in pictures.

After investigating the precise nature of the Aztec idol which lies
under the Catholic altars of Mexico, attended by kneeling pilgrims
who still gather to worship not the appearance but the true holy
substance concealed beneath the appearance, Miss Brenner ranges
the present scene gathering all elements together in the grand hope
of proving an inner spiritual unity between the ancient Indian of
Mexico, the current revolutionary program and, above all, the perfect
validity of that revolution in art once called the Mexican Renascence,
though I doubt if the label still persists there.

In the course of this procedure, done in obedience to many inner
and external compulsions, almost in spite of this tremendous effort
to reconcile all things, Miss Brenner has written a really beautiful
book. She interprets symbols in terms of human life, describes the
now-famous mural paintings of the Syndicate of Painters and Sculptors in a lively intelligible painters' jargon, and devotes a series of
remarkably fresh and delightful biographical chapters to individual
painters who helped to make the most exciting period of art in the
history of America. The chapter on the syndicate conveys the breathless commotion of those few years in Mexico when the new way of
painting progressed in Mexico in a whirlwind of manifestos, public demonstrations, newspaper campaigns, with adolescent mob violence expending itself on the still unfinished murals and respectable
ladies demanding that the vile pictures be covered over before they
would consent to hold a meeting in the patio of the preparatory
school. Art occupied no ivory tower, but rolled in the dust of conflict with local politics, religion and the agrarian question and came

out victorious, for the walls are there, covered with the simple and irrefutable testimony that once, for a short time, a group of extraordinary artists collaborated in producing works of art.

The artists in Mexico followed the revolution and their activities occurred at the end of a period, not at a beginning, as most of them involved in it wished to believe. In the first part of the decade between 1910 and 1921 several good artists, now well known, were working in obscurity—floating particles lost in the confusion, as were the artists of Russia during the first years of readjustment from 1917. The artists returned to Mexico at the first promise of peace—for they were nearly all abroad—and though they took their color from the political and economic atmosphere, still they came late and their revolution was the crowning pyrotechnical display that marked the end of the long groaning process of political change.

Still they were revolutionists and in a sense above politics, for they recognized, they exhumed from under the debris of extraneous hostile life, the art of the Indian in Mexico, and they restored the Indian himself, a perpetual exile in his own land, to the status of a human problem before a world that had almost ceased to regard that race as a living force in Mexico. They fought the enemies of their idea within the walls and without. They adopted habits of thought, and adapted methods of working, and went, in the process, very consciously "primitive," imitating the Indian miracle paintings, delving among ruins, searching in the archives, attending Indian fiestas, using the native earths for their colors. They talked among themselves, compared findings, defending each his own point of view, and ended, evidently, in confirming one another's discoveries in all essentials. The Indian was the only real artist in America, they said, and they proved it by pointing to his serapes, his jugs, his ex-votos, his pulqueria decorations and his way of living. They discarded awareness for the darker, profounder current of instinct, which when followed faithfully, did not, they believed, betray. They rejected the mechanistic devices for keeping the surfaces of life in motion and plunged boldly to the depths of the "unconscious."

This led to a remarkable paradox.

Dr. Manuel Gamio, the anthropologist, who has devoted his life to the cause of Indian life in Mexico, is a Spaniard, Mexican born. Jose Vasconcelos, then Minister of Education, who fostered the work of the Syndicate of Painters and Sculptors, is Spanish-Mexican. Siqueiros, Mexican born, who furnished the theory of action for the syndicate and organized it, was sent to Europe by the Carranza government to study. Adolfo Best-Maugard, who created a method of design based on Aztec motives, is Spanish-French, educated in Europe. Jean Charlot is mostly French and Parisian. Merida is a Guatemalan, who in Europe was associated with Modigliani. Dr. Atl, one of the true pioneers, is partly German. Diego Rivera is a Mexican-born Spaniard, who spent sixteen years in Europe, following the erratic course of modern painting in many capitals. Some of these have a tinge of Jewish blood, others have Indian blood. The great renascence of Indian art was a movement of mestizos and foreigners who found in Mexico, simultaneously, a direction they could take toward extended boundaries. They respected the fruitful silence of the Indian and they shouted for this silence at the top of their lungs.

Those of us in Mexico at the time saw this happen: that not one pure-blooded Indian artist contributed his motivating force to initiate this movement. Several of them joined in, but of the active men not one but had fled out of Europe with years of training and experience, saturated with theories and methods, bent on fresh discoveries. This excepts Orozco and a prodigious child, Abraham Angel, who learned from his elders, then surpassed them in a single leap, and died at nineteen years. Xavier Guerrero, a full-blooded Indian, joined the syndicate, kept his silence and did magnificent work. When he wished to articulate a faith he edited a Communist periodical, in itself a work of art. For him his way of painting sprang from no intellectual or sentimental atavism; it was a simple continuing. He wasted no words on it.

The non-Indians made the experiments and did the explaining.

The famous Syndicate of Painters and Sculptors, with Diego Rivera as a storm center, presented a front of formidable solidarity to the hostile public and fought ferociously among themselves because communality of work and idea can be won only by endless war. The younger artists admired Diego, imitated his work without shame, and ended by convincing themselves that they had worked in that method from the cradle. They revolted against this top-heavy personality which threatened the balance of the group and drew caricatures of Diego, swathed monumentally in a Ku-Klux Klan sheet, shoving them into graves and pushing earth over them. But they held together and followed him just the same.

If the syndicate painters purified the atmosphere of the more obvious picturesqueness already exploited sickeningly by their immediate predecessors, still they found their reality ready to hand. The Indian sat, a complete design in space, ready for them. The painters learned soberly and did not corrupt the thing they found. All the symbols are preserved intact. For example, as Miss Brenner notes, ancient symbol of the hand with the flower; this appears over again, and the laboring hand is esteemed a thing of marvelous beauty; great hands of war clasped over a sword hilt; hands grasping a machete, molding a pot; wearing, digging in the mines, delving in the earth, scattering the seeds; this laboring hand became a vast basic symbol. Tina Modotti, an Italian, makes photographs of hands and has made a beautiful study of the hands of Amado Galvan, the potter, for this book, and so united were the artists, no matter what their medium, and so faithful were they to their visions, Tina Modotti's photographs from life appear at first glance to be photographs of Diego's paintings.

I wish some one as well equipped for the work might do for the United States of North America what Miss Brenner has done for Mexico. Surely this country, which exhibits such special and florid contradictions, such gargantuan appetites, such magnificence of crime, architecture and machinery, might also be discovered to have some common, unifying source. Explained in terms of creative vitality and racial intermixtures, we might find ourselves justified in being "with pleasure and talent" Americans. We practice to a degree the "vacilada" which Miss Brenner defines as the loud laughter meant to conceal, but which reveals the waverings of despair induced by the necessity to face tragedy without signs of fear. Miss

Brenner says this is very Mexican, very mestizo. It would be simpler
to say it is very human and excessively Western. What else is the
Italian farce? What else the *Merry Wives of Windsor*? The Punch
and Judy show? Our own comic strip for the sake of which large
numbers of persons buy the newspapers? In Mexico, true, they are
immensely vivid in everything, and in spite of her hatred for the
"picturesque," for that word is rightly outlaw, Miss Brenner is more
than once captured and misled by this definitely Mexican talent for
high visibility. Why not? It is one of their attractions.

Miss Brenner distributes honors among the painters by a somewhat incalculable system of estimates, and I rather finished her book
feeling that if one admired Orozco, then it was not quite possible to
give high rank to Diego Rivera. The witty and talented Jean Charlot
receives as much attention as either of these important figures, and
there are other mysterious selections and exclusions. But in the end
this is a book about Mexico not to be missed—a stimulating record of
a vital period in the history of American art told by a contemporary
eyewitness.

✍ The Fair-Haired Man

New York Herald Tribune Books, November 3, 1929, pp. 1–2.

Review of *The Gothick North, A Study of Medieval Life, Art and Thought*,
by Sacheverell Sitwell (Boston: Houghton Mifflin Company, 1929).

There is more to this book than the mere reading of it, for it is stipu-
lated that you must also witness its creation line by line. You will
find nothing of the surly literary hermit in Mr. Sitwell. He is like a
busy sculptor surrounded by friends watching him work, while he
hacks and chisels away, talking all the while about what he is doing
now, and what he means to do next.

Mr. Sitwell explains first that a poet cannot forever be writing
poetry, and in the necessary intervals the denser levels of prose offer
the perfect medium for keeping his faculties in trim. Prose demands

a subject, and choosing one is always difficult, for the possibilities are numerous even when guided by a natural preference for a theme not tarnished by too much handling. After long meditation Mr. Sitwell chose the cold clear morning time of the Gothick North, because the present trend of taste is firmly set against this peculiar period; this incited him to study its massive remains and discover the survivals of its spirit, in order to re-estimate its values, defend its virtues and extol its beauties. Thus he effects a double escape: from the banalities of current intellectual dogma and from the personal peril of being labelled, once for all, as the author of *Southern Baroque Art.*

Prefacing his study of medieval life, art and thought, Mr. Sitwell does a true public service by denouncing the modern painter and the picture critics, who by being strident and mediocre have got the upper hand of public opinion in a way that effectually blocks the education of that helpless body. He notes in passing that the worst of painters—and in England they are very, very bad—sells his worst picture for a better price than the best of poets receives for his soundest poem. This is true, it has always been true, and it is very discouraging.

Many other just grievances and accumulated indignations keep getting in Mr. Sitwell's way as the book begins. Miss Corder, his first art teacher, crosses the commons of his childhood memories for a season of Fridays, causing him to recast the whole shape of his plan at a critical moment. Professing his interest in the present, above all periods, he finds it full of unprepossessing things which continually hinder his journey into the past, and equally forbid him to live reconciled to his time. There can be no forgiveness, in his new mood, for the "ugly obscurity which passes for modern in so much of the music and painting of our day"; nor for machines, noises, advertising, speed, the cinema, and so on. Most of these horrors were generated in America, England's bloated stepchild. He hates America, almost he fears that crouching, blind, insensate monster, fecund of barbarisms. For present technical purposes it is necessary to be in flight from all this, but there can be no true escape, so Mr. Sitwell compromises by a system of alternations and transitions, of "present fictions accompanying a created past." In the middle of the book, marking a division in mood and pointing a new direction, there occur two chapters of fiction, "At the Play" and "Love Scene." The second is described as "a transcendentalized account" of a "lived or merely written adventure," which the poet playfully hopes will "put some of the novelists in their places."

The rest is praise for the tall, fair-haired man, who, encased in his armor like a turtle in his carapace, created that vertical civilization which cast its heavy shadow over all Europe. It was a gross cold race which believed it sprang from itself alone; and rooted its family pride in a mythical genealogy. It had no memory, and therefore no history; it was without music and without poetry, its love songs were mere nursery jingles and its emotions swung incessantly between "two states of terror and exaltation, of panic and rhapsody." Barbarians, in a word, delighting in startling disproportions in architecture, distortions of the human body by means of dress, perversion of human life by savagely inflicted limitations. Yet by sheer blind will they overlaid all the other races of their world.

Owning the imperfections of that Frankish age, Mr. Sitwell proposes to engage in a long reverie, dwelling upon its beauties. This must be done while traveling in several dimensions, and by disregarding the three rude divisions of time. To this end he groups his characters arbitrarily, whether fictional, living, historical, or evoked from stone and tapestry; he brings together the most dissimilar scenes, moving at the most diverse speeds, in most widely separated periods, inhabiting multiple planes of experience, and fuses them into harmony. It cost him, he admits, infinite and dolorous labor, and why should we be unmindful of his pains?

Even so, the past cannot be made to live again; it cannot be seen clearly or truly understood; but there are surviving fragments fit to excite the imagination. Tapestries may be washed in a mystical river, and the little figures in it will dance under water with a fleeting illusion of life. Knights and ladies may stroll on the decorated panels of a marriage chest. Pious wedded pairs still kneel at their devotions in the leaves of illuminated Books of Hours; knights give battle in a wood on a narrow strip of embroidery; monks gorge themselves at dinner, but only in a painting; hunting horns blow in a dream. . . .

The horn is a danger signal of which one must be careful. The past is inhabited by the demon of romance, and the poet must tread circumspectly in fear of that ominous shade. During a detailed, perfected, lyrical description of the Chatsworth hunting tapestries he is almost carried away by "the ancient traditional pomp" which "has something in it which strikes an inherited importance and terror into the heart of the beholder." It is time to pull up. He adds: "The hunting horn, preluding far in front of the main body, announces the procession riding away in the shadows. The romantic poets of a century ago throw open their casements, pull on their doublets, and comb their long, troubled hair, for this is a dream come true." In spite of this happy device for shifting the responsibility, one feels that they still precede Mr. Sitwell merely by 100 years. But no matter. Mr. Sitwell has the added quality of modernity, which provides levity at the right moment, and takes the curse off rapture.

It must be a curse, he guards against it so carefully. When the momentum of his reverie is not broken by the rattle of a shutter, or the clatter of the housemaid's broom in the hall at a moment of sheer flight, there are other pre-arranged signals for calling a halt and taking a more level place. There are always Miss Corder and her brother Carl.

"This peculiar pair of spiritual witnesses had contrived their arrival at the very moment it was best calculated to dispel any illusions that might have gathered during their absence." Their yearning shades haunt him wherever he turns, and threaten to spoil his finest effects. He enters a cathedral, and lets himself go in long brilliant passages of shining, flexible prose, studded like stars with lovely names of artists dead and gone, weighted with judgments and comparisons, fairly singing with emotions—and there they are before him, in his fiction of their destiny, doing Europe on a belated legacy, dogging his path with sketchbooks. Sadder than the ruins they love, deader than the dead past they adore so blindly, they intervene between him and the crumbling walls which he had meant to festoon with life-giving words, drawing precisely what they see with their two pairs of eyes, and doing it very badly, too. They hate the present worse than he does, even to omnibuses and Virginia tobacco. They are a godsend to

Mr. Sitwell. He uses their pathetic, shopworn point of view as a lever to draw himself back to the indispensable sophisticated detachment; they purify him of the commonplace.

As in the "Love Scene" Mr. Sitwell seems more cheerfully at home in his own period than he cares to admit, so in the chapter on monasteries, where he is less mindful of his thesis, less occupied with stratagems for derailing himself, and more objectively concerned with comparative histories, he is more at his ease, and more effective. Here, indeed, is a poet making holiday with prose, and no doubt putting any number of persons in their places.

✍ Bohemian Futility

New Masses, 5 (November 1929), pp. 15–16.

Review of *Money for Love*, by Josephine Herbst
(New York: Coward-McCann, 1929).

In her second novel, Josephine Herbst strips her vocabulary to fighting trim and goes for poor lost middle western human nature with a kind of cold detached ferocity that makes my hair rise. When she has finished, I am inclined to cry, "Better never to have been born if this were all!" Yet while I would like to argue with her on the grounds that I never met any people quite like this, I have to admit they do exist, for she has created them. Without apologies or explanations, without pity, Miss Herbst states the case of a set of young, half-endowed, once-hopeful men and women who came to New York to do great things, and for one reason or another, died, one by one, on their feet. The thing is done so simply, so perfectly, in such an even tempo, and with such disconcerting calmness on the part of the author, you will be tempted almost to believe that nothing much is happening. At the end, and this is not a happy ending, you realize that a miniature drama of crime, with blackmail, adultery, and a half dozen cross plots of betrayal, has been played to its logical end of frustration for each of the confused, self-engrossed plotters. You see, they are all really such nice young people—or would have been if only they had not all needed money so badly. All of them are presumably in good health, they have youth and good looks, they come from sound decent God-fearing middle western families, and each one is intelligent enough to have made a start in such specialized professions as chemistry, medicine, and the theatre, but none of them knows how to go about getting the money they need to finish with.

They meet up in New York and form one of those aimless, accidental group associations, and get involved gradually in each other's affairs, which they confide in monosyllabic phrases in blind pigs over beer and synthetic whisky. Each one wishes he were somewhere else, or with some one else, or could get along a little more smoothly with the others, but this is impossible, because they are all scared, and distrust one another, with rather good reason, as it turns out. They are not really criminals, they are young people determined to live according to the code they half-believe in: Love is so much tripe and honor is a romantic word, and what it takes to get on in this world is money . . . My God, where to get it? For they know nothing of finance, economics, they have no inheritance to look forward to, and when they work they do not earn enough. So in their weakness they are cruel, and commit unpardonable petty crimes against each other continually, and they blunder around until you want to shake them.

Harriet, the most living creature of them all, is an actress on the road to Broadway success, but her real vocation is love, and her true ambition—a perfectly womanly one, not to be despised—is to be successful with men. Alas in her race for sophistication she attempts to take a married man away from his wife. This man, made up of "obscene timidity," a yearning for extra-marital adventure during his wife's recurring seasons of gestation, and a grand faith in conventional bourgeois morals, is the only one who plays double and wins. He betrays his wife to his mistress and his mistress to his wife, profiting by the emotional vanity of both, and comes out even. He is the only one who does.

Harriet, having failed with him, and failed in the theatre because of the unhappiness she suffered through him, blackmails him for $5000 in order to help her present lover, who wants to study medicine in Vienna. He sends her forty dollars. There follows a dreadful little struggle between them, and she succeeds, after a humiliating episode, in wringing $1000 from him. There remains only to bind her present lover, who is half in love with another girl. I have the feeling that the only true satisfaction Harriet got out of the whole affair was her pretty new hat, the first buy with her blood-money. No one could call her a victor.

The others are not in much better case, but we won't go into that.

The story is nothing much, and these people are less than nothing, but they are terrible in their nothingness, and you observe them finally with the most acute sensations of pity and horror because they are like fishes trapped in an aquarium, swimming round and round . . . What good would it do them to have money? Suppose they did work at their professions, where would they end? What if they do so-to-speak fall in love? Even their few sexual adventures are half-hearted, bleak, joyless. The maternal Elsie, wife of Harriet's former lover, is only a Harriet who married young. It is a poor, faithless, worthless marriage, but it is hers, and so she accepts all indignities and has her complacent little moments of triumph, forgiving her husband his tasteless escapades.

No. These people are more interesting in this book than they were before, or could be again. They are fascinating in a fearful way, because a good artist, perfectly in command of her method, has for her own mysterious reasons chosen to assemble them: her lack of human pity is her own business. She has made a fine job of destruction. What, precisely, is she trying to kill?

✍ The Most Catholic King

New York Herald Tribune Books, December 1, 1929, p. 5.

Review of *King Spider. Some Aspects of Louis XI of France*, by D. B. Wyndham Lewis (New York: Coward-McCann, 1929).

As described in his preface to this study of King Louis XI of France, Mr. Lewis's attitude toward historical research and the work of biographers is so entirely admirable it might serve as a model for all historians. First, he refuses to do again what has been done well, and so leaves the solid biography and chronicle to M. Pierre Champion. He makes no attempt to compare legend with historical fact, for that task has been completed by Mr. Orville Mosher. He confines his researches to "contemporary and authentic sources alone," drawing alike on the testimony of friends and enemies, to display a series of arresting lifelike pictures of a little long-nosed, crooked-legged man whom Jehan Molinet, poet, called "the universal Spider." He has concerned himself with real history, and, citing a dignified list of documents, somewhat peevishly gives us his word of honor that he has read them all: "There is no fiction here. Where there is conversation it is not imagined, but recorded; where there are descriptions of men or things they are similarly authentic and unadorned." He has refused, on failing to find a motive, to invent one. He has done away with footnotes out of courtesy to the reader. He makes deduction but seldom, and then only lawfully in accordance with the evidence, for he has no personal prejudices to serve, "or any private mullygrub of the mind."

In fact, this book is a warm apology for King Louis XI of France, written by a romantically fervent Catholic who is also a devoted antiquarian, who intersperses his authentic history with hymns of praise for the church, for the blessed fifteenth century, for its music, its poetry, its customs, its laws, its spirit. It is done with devotion, a beautiful fullness of reference, a splendid marshaling of the evidence to support the author's preference for that glorious Catholic monarchical age. As a work of research and arrangement it is admirable, but is spoiled when Mr. Lewis falls, as he did in his life of François Villon, into a sentimental, almost tearful, religiosity, alternated with outbursts of bullying and irrelevant personal opinions of the cursed present times in which we are doomed to live. As a christened Catholic, I find myself irritated by all this. It seems quite unnecessary. It does not seem quite Catholic in the proper sense.

Mr. Lewis sneers at modern scientific knowledge, and explains seriously that King Louis undoubtedly drew in his ferocious love of the land of France with the milk of his peasant wet-nurse; and ever after exhibited the avaricious meanness and the gross tastes of a peasant. He is embittered because the modern financial world—of England at least—is in the grip of Levantine financiers, yet it was good King Louis who first protected the Jewish bankers, and, using their special genius for his own ends, set the Jews firmly on their way to power in Europe. On the heels of sarcasm for our own invaluable Mr. Henry Ford, with his deadly efficiency, he defends the perfect modernistic efficiency of King Louis XI, who built roads and opened markets, encouraged the silk industry, organized a postal service throughout the kingdom and bargained like a horse jobber with kings, nobles, merchants, friends, enemies, and even with Our Lady, who got a fine church in exchange for a victory over the English.

Even as Mr. Lewis bewails with the fervor of a preaching friar the noisome evils of this present generation, he quotes long passages from the preaching friars of the fifteenth century who rebuked the court for its scandals and nagged at the women for dressing frivolously, painting their faces, starving themselves for a slim figure and shunning maternity. King Louis took the sensible, short way with these pests. If he could not shut them up he banished them. Why, since Mr. Lewis approves so heartily of the works of this king, should he be so appalled if their effects still persist and expand?

King Louis XI was a figure of supreme importance in the history of fifteenth-century Europe. He made the hundred years' peace with England to balance the hundred years' war. He was one of the important agents in the breaking down of the feudal system, and, pious son of the church militant that he was, he fought even the Pope, if it was a question of money, power or the advantage of France. He found France a clutter of warring dukedoms, and he left it a soundly united kingdom. His method was to keep his court, his whole country, a "spider's nest" of intrigue. He went to war only when he could not possibly avoid it and bought off his enemies instead. He believed that money would buy anything, and he received full proof that he was right. Only one man is on record as refusing to be bought, Thomas Basin, Bishop of Lisieux, and him Louis hounded almost to the grave.

Diplomacy with him was a word used to cover a vast network of treacheries. He betrayed the loyal city of Liège to the Duke of Burgundy in order to save his own skin, but he always kissed the altarcloth when he received holy communion. He gathered about him as gorgeous a crew of knaves as ever served a king and made them rich on stolen lands and offices, where they were at liberty to plunder his beloved people to their hearts' content. He gave rich gifts to famous shrines until the Cardinal Archbishop of Tours rebuked him, saying "it would be better to give less money to shrines and endeavor to lighten the burden of taxation on his people instead." He plotted against his father, King Charles VII, and when called to account coolly attempted to blame his faithful friend and counsellor, Antoine de Chabannes, Comte de Dammartin. He hated his first wife, and for thirty-four years after her death refused to spend 600 crowns to bury her in the church she had named in her will as her desired resting place; and he was stingy with his mistresses. In all the crowded record there is not one relation, whether diplomatic, religious or personal, that he did not dishonor. Yet he possessed the qualities necessary for his appointed work—complete unscrupulousness, effectiveness in action, a definite air and a tyrant's will. With such a man it is enough to tell the story of his life. There is no need to apologize for him by saying that he went on pilgrimages and died in the odor of sanctity.

✍ These Pictures Must Be Seen

New York Herald Tribune Books, December 22, 1929, p. 5.

Review of *The Frescoes of Diego Rivera*, with an introduction by
Ernestine Evans (New York: Harcourt, Brace and Company, 1929).

For seven years, during a period of more than ordinarily ecstatic turbulence in the life of his native country, the frescoes of Diego Rivera have been spreading, with the power and persistence of an organic growth, upon the walls of public buildings in Mexico. After sixteen

years of experiment and discovery in Europe he went home and proceeded to make the question of art an issue as immediate, disturbing
and almost as dangerous as a Presidential election. He was a veteran
of the series of campaigns which followed cubism after 1912, and his
mission to Mexico was not one of peace. In politics he was a revolutionary. Painters sprang up around him by the dozen, for luckily
all the good ones were also radical, at least in theory. The mediocre
ones stuck by the Academy and the good old times. There was a grati-
fying amount of seething and ferment, during which his syndicate
of painters and sculptors produced some of the best modern painting, if not sculpture, to be found in the world. Rivera, because of his
phenomenal personality and his absolute mastery of the situation,
was in danger of becoming a legend, a symbol, before his work was
half finished. His followers have for him a warmth of adulation little
short of worship. His enemies are positively worth having.

It is almost impossible to exaggerate the excitements, the disorders
of the life around him when he began his frescoes, or the pressure
under which he worked. The group he had gathered shattered from
within and dispersed after the first year. Rivera remained alone and
painted. Except for two visits to Russia, where he worked for short
periods, he moved from the walls of the Ministry of Education to the
National Preparatory School in Mexico City, and from thence to the
National Agricultural Academy in Chapingo. The mere volume of
his labors is impressive, a testimony to the singleness of his idea, and
the union of his individual mind with the tradition which formed it.

Tough fibered and resistant, he is an emotional revolutionist, and
when he explains his social beliefs in words it comes down pretty
fairly to a simple philosophic anarchy, such as almost any Spaniard
might express. Within the province of his art all is complete harmony,
order, obedience. He selected a difficult, uncompromising medium
and proceeded to inclose his intractable material within the confines
of a formal beauty. For him the enormous confusion of the visible
world can be reduced to a study in geometrical balance, sober color
and cross rhythms suspended at the moment of precise harmony. The
vision is grand and simple, a little too bucolic, maybe, at times a
trifle inflated; but I believe he is the most important living painter.

We are indebted to Miss Ernestine Evans for this first collection of photographs of the murals and an interesting introduction to the artist. The reproductions are very fine and preserve to a degree the values of the subdued grays, brick reds, silvery greens and deep blues of the paintings. The color is secondary, for Rivera emphasizes structure and rhythm. It is a very timely and valuable book.

✍ A Disinherited Cosmopolitan

New York Herald Tribune Books, February 16, 1930, p. 22.

Review of *Essays on American Literature*, by Lafcadio Hearn
(Kanda, Tokyo, Japan: Jokuseido Press, 1929).

It is always a temptation to over-value half-finished things that promised well, and one feels the same elegiac piety for the memory of a frustrated artist that one feels for children who die in their first years of promise. It is perfectly useless to speculate on the possible achievements of a man like Lafcadio Hearn, if he had had a more fortunate life. His history is fragmentary, his literary remains are mere fragments, yet a small number of devoted friends, American and Japanese, resolutely keep his memory alive because, after a quarter of a century, they find him still irreplaceable. Albert Mordell, of Philadelphia, and Sanki Ichikawa, of the Tokio Imperial University, have chosen to mark the twenty-fifth anniversary of his death by publishing this collection of newspaper and magazine articles written by Hearn during his life in New Orleans, from 1878 to 1887.

Hearn was born homeless, lived a wanderer, and died while a guest in the house of his friends, and his history is a series of flights from one intolerable situation into another, except for a brief period of comparative adjustment in Japan. His father was an English soldier who married a Greek woman in Leucadia, and Hearn named himself for this island which he never saw after his early childhood there. He was a thin-skinned creature, with an unstable set of nerves, and he could not swallow an English education, nor find a spiritual foothold in the Roman Catholic faith, in which he was christened.

At nineteen years, casting himself upon a world with no idea of how he might survive, he came to America, where his sufferings were atrocious. He picked up a casual existence here and there, married a mulatto woman in Cincinnati, lost her somehow along the way and arrived in New Orleans almost a derelict. With the peculiar optimism of a neurotic, he attempted to run a restaurant in this city of famous restaurants, failed, and took to newspaper writing, being employed by *The Item* and *The Times-Democrat.*

During his dislocated early period he had prepared himself for the work, and his view of America and American literature was cast on a background of developed taste for and knowledge of the French Romantics. He hated Naturalism as expounded by Zola and Puritanism as preached by William Dean Howells, and he had a rather undifferentiated admiration for Henry James, Mark Twain and George W. Cable. Of the then popular writers, he saw through such as Bret Harte without much trouble, was a little more than just to Joaquin Miller, and praised gloriously two or three authors whose names are now dust. At this period he was no more than a poverty-stricken hack, afraid of his job, and his judgments, necessarily hasty, by necessity written in haste, were none the less in many cases true, delicate and intense, and if they seem a little worn by now it is because they have become familiar by adoption. They were new then, and even bold. Only once did he fail himself. When ordered to attack Whitman violently he did it, and the evidence rather points to his genuine aversion for Whitman; but he explained privately to Whitman admirers that it was not possible to praise him in a newspaper meant for family circulation.

New Orleans, with its half dozen closely mingled races and languages, was the kindest atmosphere he could find in this country; but it was not very kind to him. He escaped to the West Indian Islands on a commission from *The Times-Democrat,* and wrote his delightful book, *Two Years in the West Indies.* Returning, he fled again, as a newspaper correspondent, to Japan, found his refuge there, broke with the newspaper and became a teacher of English at the University of Tokio. It was his good fortune that he arrived at the beginning of the Japanese expansion into world affairs, and ironically he became interpreter between two civilizations equally alien to him. He chose to know Japan. Eagerly he took part in the ceremonies of citizenship in this hospitable land, so fantastic to his eye, so solidly and realistically ordered to his mind. He was naturalized, took a Japanese name, became a Buddhist, married a Japanese wife, raised about himself all possible barriers against human relationship and for seven years devoted himself to explaining English literature to the Japanese and the Japanese spirit to the West. These lectures survive only in the notes taken at class by his students and published as *A History of English Literature*. It is true pioneer work, and in it Hearn discloses that he loved fixed values, a secure and formal existence, a moral code on the grand style, finalities; no wonder the Japanese did not find him very surprising, but accepted him as one of them for good and all. Truth is, they ended by understanding him better than he did them, and as he labored to interpret them to the West while he lived, now with memorable courtesy they continue to interpret him to the world where he lived as a disinherited man.

✍ Example to the Young

New Republic, vol. 66, no. 855 (April 22, 1931), pp. 279–80.

Review of *Wedding Day and Other Stories*, by Kay Boyle (New York: Jonathan Cape and Harrison Smith, 1930); and *Plagued by the Nightingale*, by Kay Boyle (New York: Jonathan Cape and Harrison Smith, 1931).

Miss Kay Boyle's way of thinking and writing stems from sources still new in the sense that they have not been supplanted. She is young enough to regard them as in the category of things past, a sign, I suppose, that she is working in a tradition and not in a school. Gertrude Stein and James Joyce were and are the glories of their time and some very portentous talents have emerged from their shadows. Miss Boyle, one of the newest, I believe to be among the strongest. At present she is identified as one of the *Transition* group, but these two books just published should put an end to that. What is a group, anyhow? In this one were included—as associate editors and contributors to *Transition*—many Americans: Harry Crosby, William Carlos Williams, Hart Crane, Matthew Josephson, Isidor Schneider, Josephine Herbst, Murray Godwin, Malcolm Cowley, John Herrman, Laura Riding—how many others?—and Miss Boyle herself. They wrote in every style under heaven and they spent quite a lot of time fighting with each other. Not one but would have resented, and rightly, the notion of discipleship or of interdependence. They were all vigorous not so much in revolt as in assertion, and most of them had admirably subversive ideas. Three magazines sustained them and were sustained by them: *Transition*, Ernest Walsh's *This Quarter* and *Broom*. The tremendous presences of Gertrude Stein and James Joyce were everywhere about them, and so far as Miss Boyle is concerned, it comes to this: that she is a part of the most important literary movement of her time.

She sums up the salient qualities of that movement: a fighting spirit, freshness of feeling, curiosity, the courage of her own attitude and idiom, a violently dedicated search for the meanings and methods of art. In these short stories and this novel there are further positive virtues of the individual temperament: health of mind, wit and the sense of glory. All these are qualities in which the novel marks an advance over the stories, as it does, too, in command of method.

The stories have a range of motive and feeling as wide as the technical virtuosity employed to carry it. Not all of them are successful. In some of the shorter ones, a straining of the emotional situation leads to stridency and incoherence. In others, where this strain is employed as a deliberate device, it is sometimes very successful— as notably in "Vacation Time," an episode in which an obsessional grief distorts and makes tragic a present situation not tragic of itself; the reality is masked by drunkenness, evaded by hysteria, and it is all most beautifully done. "On the Run" is a bitter story of youth in literal flight from death, which gains on it steadily; but the theme deserved better treatment.

In such stories as "Episode in the Life of an Ancestor" and "Uncle Anne," there are the beginnings of objectiveness, a soberer, richer style; and the sense of comedy, which is like acid sometimes, is here gayer and more direct. In "Portrait" and "Polar Bears and Others," Miss Boyle writes of love not as if it were a disease, or a menace, or a soothing syrup to vanity, or something to be peered at through a microscope, or the fruit of original sin, or a battle between the sexes, or a bawdy pastime. She writes as one who believes in love and romance—not the "faded flower in a buttonhole," but love so fresh and clear it comes to the reader almost as a rediscovery in literature. It was high time someone rediscovered it. There are other stories, however—"Spring Morning," "Letters of a Lady," "Episode in the Life of an Ancestor"—in which an adult intelligence plays with destructive humor on the themes of sexual superstition and pretenses between men and women. "Madame Tout Petit," "Summer," "Theme" and "Bitte Nehmen Sie die Blumen" are entirely admirable, each one a subtle feat in unraveling a complicated predicament of the human heart. "Wedding Day," the title story, is the least satisfactory, displaying the weakness of Miss Boyle's strength in a lyricism that is not quite poetry.

The novel, *Plagued by the Nightingale,* has the same germinal intensity as the shorter works, but it is sustained from the first word to the last by a sure purpose and a steadier command of resources. The form, structure and theme are comfortably familiar. The freshness and brilliancy lie in the use of the words and the point of view.

It is the history of an American girl married to a young Frenchman, and living for a short period in the provinces with his wealthy bourgeois family. There is Papa, a blustering old fool, though Bridget never says it quite so plainly; Maman, a woman of energy, good will and appalling force of character; three unmarried sisters, Annick, Julie and Marthe; Charlotte the eldest sister, married to her cousin; Pierre the elder brother, a young doctor; and Nicholas, Bridget's husband. A taint in the blood causes eccentrics and paralytics to blossom like funeral wreaths in every generation. Nicholas is warned by his weakened legs that the family disease is likely to be the main portion of his inheritance. He is dependent on his people, his wife is dowerless. Charlotte's husband is little better than an imbecile, but he is wealthy. Uncle Robert, a perverse old maid of a man, is also wealthy, and he amuses himself by tampering with family affairs; the victims endure him in the hope that he may give someone money sometime. First and last it is the question of money that agitates the family bosom.

The three younger daughters are waiting, each in her own way, for a proposal of marriage from Luc, an idolized young doctor, who nonchalantly enjoys the privilege of the devoted family without asking to become a member. Bridget is a vigorous personality, with powerful hates and loves, a merciless eye, and a range of prejudices which permits no offense against her secret faiths to be trivial. She has gayety and charm, and at first she is ingenuously fond of this household of persons so closely and tenderly bound, so united in their aims. Nicholas feels quite otherwise. He hates his dear good sweet people who are so warmly kind in small things, so hideously complacent and negligent in the larger essentials. He needs help, restitution really, from this family that has brought him disabled into the world. His father brutally—that is to say, with the utmost fatherly kindness—tells Nicholas that he will give him fifty thousand francs when Bridget has a child. Charlotte's five beautiful children are weak in the legs, but they are "the joy of existence" none the less. One's duty is to procreate for the family, however maimed the lives may be.

Bridget, caught in a whirling undercurrent of love and hatred and family intrigue, begins first to fear and then to despise these strangers as she realizes the ignoble motives back of all the family devotion. She sees her husband gradually growing hostile to her as he identifies her with his family, no longer with himself. She is confirmed in her instinctive distrust of situations and feelings sanctified by the rubber stamps of time and custom; she defends herself by mockery and the mental reservation against the blind cruelties and wrongs which are done under cover of love. Luc complicates matters by falling in love with her instead of asking for one of the sisters, but even so he does not speak until it is too late—until it is safe for him to speak, when marriage to one of the sisters is no longer the best investment he can make. And Bridget, who has wavered, been pulled almost to pieces by the tearing, gnawing, secretive antagonisms and separate aims of the family, comes to her conclusion—a rather bitter one, which in the end will solve very badly the problem. Of her own will she takes to herself the seed of decay.

This is no more than a bare and disfiguring outline of the plan of the novel. The whole manner of the telling is superb: there are long passages of prose which crackle and snap with electric energy, episodes in which inner drama and outward events occur against scenes bright with the vividness of things seen by the immediate eye: the bathing party on the beach, the fire in the village, the delicious all-day excursion to Castle Island, the scene in the market when Bridget and Nicholas quarrel, the death of Charlotte, the funeral. Nothing is misplaced or exaggerated, and the masterful use of symbol and allegory clarify and motivate the main great theme beneath the apparent one: the losing battle of youth and strength against the resistless army of age and death. This concept is implicit in the story itself, and it runs like music between the lines. The book is a magnificent performance; and as the short stories left the impression of reservoirs of power hardly tapped, so this novel, complete as it is, seems only a beginning.

✍ History on the Wing

New Republic, vol. 89, no. 1146 (November 18, 1936), p. 82.

Review of *The Stones Awake: A Novel of Mexico*, by Carleton Beals (Philadelphia: J. B. Lippincott Company, 1936).

Shortly before my last visit to Mexico, 1930–31, Carleton Beals, with several friends of his, looked over the roof ledge of his apartment and saw several strange men coming in, as it proved, to arrest him. They took him away very quietly and popped him into jail and kept him incommunicado for an uncomfortable length of time. Mr. Beals, who rarely confuses himself with the hero of his own works, was bored and angry and nervous all at once, being uncertain whether they meant to shoot him. He persuaded himself that it seemed unlikely. In the meantime, they had interrupted several books, articles and journeys of his, all of which have been finished since, and dozens more. His arrest had been ordered by a certain politician, really a quite dangerous thug, who objected to Mr. Beals's truthful and therefore damaging account of the politician's life and works. Why he let Mr. Beals go again I do not remember, but I imagine he is regretting it. Mr. Beals has gone on his cheerful career of gathering, arranging more or less neatly and publishing great floods of damaging, disrespectful truths about Mexico's corrupt politicians ever since. Side by side with this tenacious labor of hatred, or rather, knotted and woven in with it, goes his labor of love: a patient, constant presentation of the life and fate of the Indians, the wronged, the disinherited, the endlessly exploited industrial and agricultural workers of Mexico.

He never fails, you know always where to find him. It must be nearly twenty years since he went to Mexico, and if he lives a hundred more he could never write all he has seen and heard and learned about the life in that most complicated and confused country. But no doubt he means to try, and if anyone of our time can get all the essentials on record, he can.

He might have been a fine novelist if he had had time to stop and learn. He could have been a frightfully overpaid newspaperman if a sensational career had been his aim. He is neither, as it happens; when he writes facts, he really sticks to the facts, and that capacity is beyond praise. But when he turns to the art of the novel, he does not stick to art, and that is a pity. He is still a first-rate reporter writing his memories, telling good stories, explaining the predicament of the Indian and rousing sympathy and indignation for him, kidnaping his characters whole and sound out of real life and setting them in the midst of real events, so that instead of marveling at their reality, you would think it odd if they didn't seem real. Of course they are real. That is why, in his scenes of absolutely private lives and relationships, Mr. Beals suffers from a failure of imagination. He cannot follow his characters into the locked doors of their hearts and minds because he did not create them. With one exception. He knows Esperanza, the Indian village girl born in peonage. She is one of the most natural, breathing, appealing women in American fiction. No doubt he has worked faithfully from a model, for knowing his methods any other assumption would be fantastic, but he knows, for once, more about a certain kind of woman than she could be apt to know about herself. And he presents her, carries her through, develops her character and mind and personality, shows her growing up, growing older, arriving at a logical point of experience, in the end, which is merely a point of departure for another cycle of experience, and she really does live on quite tangibly after the book is closed.

This is a feat; how it happens I do not know, in the jungle of episode, the confusion of political crime and constant revolution, the crowds of characters and changes of scene. You will learn a great deal about Mexico from any one of Mr. Beals's books, whether novel or chronicle of that country. But you can know Esperanza only by reading *The Stones Awake.* She is worth knowing.

✍ Rivera's Personal Revolution in Mexico

New York Herald Tribune Books, March 21, 1937, p. 7.

Review of *Portrait of Mexico,* paintings by Diego Rivera, text by
Bertram D. Wolfe (New York: Covici-Friede, 1937).

Portrait of Mexico might well be the good, honest final job destined to end books about Mexico. Or maybe that is only cheerful wishthinking on the part of this reviewer.

There is—or was, for friendships collapse as swiftly as other things in Mexico—a long and firm bond between the collaborators on this book: personal and esthetic sympathies, similarity of political belief, and a shared continuous loving preoccupation with Mexico. This has resulted happily in a sound book, giving for the first time in my experience an inclusive and coherent history of Mexico from preconquest days to the present, and a key to the work of Diego Rivera, not only as painter but as pictorial historian of Mexico, the land and its people.

Mr. Wolfe is the typical international Jew, born student and reformer, a man without a country save as he adopts it; even then, as we see at present in Germany, he is always in peril of finding himself homeless. Still, this capacity for choice makes for a special kind of patriotism, as for instance in Mr. Wolfe, based on love and attention and a desire to know one's chosen country really. Mr. Wolfe has the keen eye and the nose for research of a first-rate reporter, and he is in fact the only man I ever trusted to give me a straight story about political and social situations as they came in Mexico. He has his own political faith, schismatic and obdurate, and this gives to his conclusions a certain slant, of course, but in the mean time he has told a dreadful story of cross-purpose and treachery and corruption which would appall and discourage a less-seasoned campaigner.

Mr. Wolfe has sorted out his mass of material and divided it into logical sections, each admirably concise and full. He finds his way deftly through the almost inextricable knot of political and personal relationships and conflicting motives of the "revolutionists" from Madero to the present Cardenas. He proves by implication rather clearly that the first step to a stable "revolutionary" government is to kill off all the real rebels as early in the game as possible. His list of honest murdered men and living crooks is impressive.

He has incorporated into this history the history of Diego Rivera as painter in Mexico, painter of Mexico, with a key to the no-doubt thousands of square yards of murals, crowded with historical faces drawn from life, from imagination, and all too often, from bad photographs or old portraits, which cover nearly all the available wall space in Mexico's public buildings. The total effect is monstrous, as is the total energy of this big slow-moving man, half hero, half mountebank, as artists sometimes are. He has been "news" in the most literal sense of the word, from the day he first mounted his scaffoldings in the Preparatoria: broadbeamed, ox eyed, wearing the costume of the day laborer and the pistols of the mestizo, and he has been "news" ever since, on this side of the world. Amid interruptions, uproar, personal battles and political ones, he has continued imperturbably at his self-appointed task: to make the walls of Mexico his monument, as once the walls of Basel were Hans Holbein's. But there is a moral here; for Hans Holbein's wall paintings have clean vanished from Basel, and his monument is elsewhere. All the more reason, then, for this book, to keep the record when all that is left of Rivera's work will be his canvases, preserved in private collections and museums.

No single man in his time has ever had more influence on the eye and mind of the public who know his work than Diego Rivera; for he has made them see his Mexico, to accept his version of it, and often to think it better than their own. This is no small feat, and indeed, the hugeness of his accomplishment is the wonder of America, given as we are to the love of minor masterpieces and the minute perfections. For myself, and I believe I speak for great numbers, Mexico does not appear to me as it did before I saw Rivera's paintings of it. The mountains, the Indians, the horses, the flowers and children, have all subtly changed in outlines and colors. They are Rivera's Indians and flowers and all now, but I like looking at them.

The photographs are good, not too brilliantly reproduced perhaps, but not misleading, they give one a very good notion of the originals. There are in these pictures—there were always, from the beginning, some stunningly beautiful spots, whole walls of painting better, I dare say, than anything else being done today. There are also long dreary stretches of plain hack-work, overcrowded, incoherent, mechanical; a breathless jostling of anachronistic characters, and too much detail, which, when shown in the large, do not justify their presence by any special beauty or excellence.

One of the best spots has been reproduced on the jacket. Rivera, for all his completely muddled politics, his childish social theories and personal opportunism, is saying, in this painting, just this: that bullets cannot destroy the spirit you see looking out of the eyes of these three men. Wolfe, much clearer and more "literate," as the special jargon of his special wing has it, backs him up with the facts. But even he is confused as to the probable results of the encroaching machine on the Indian, agrarian, manual worker, primitive communist. He ends his valuable study on the conventional note of hope for a new dawn, and soon; a hope so rosy one would like to share it, and so vague one does not know where to begin. It seems, in this book, to be based on the expectation of an organized and expertly directed revolt of the Indian peasant and worker, and bestows upon them, for the future, a capacity for unity and steadiness of purpose they have not shown in the past. According to Mr. Wolfe's own findings, the Indian social system was decayed with class war, religious tyranny, social injustice, even when Cortés found them. There was, it would seem, revolution in Mexico, even then.

✍ Dulce et Decorum Est

New Republic, vol. 90, no. 1165 (March 31, 1937), pp. 244–45.

Review of *None Shall Look Back*, by Caroline Gordon (New York: Charles Scribner's Sons, 1937).

Fontaine Allard, tobacco planter, slave holder full of cares and responsibilities, an old man walking in a part of his Kentucky woods, "had a strange feeling, as if a voice said to him, 'these are your father's and your fathers' before him' . . . he had actually for a moment been overcome by his attachment for that earth, those trees." This is in the beginning of *None Shall Look Back*. Toward the end, his son Ned returns from the lost war, a skeleton, a dying man. "The land's still there, I reckon," he says, and goes back to it, hoping to live, but certain at least that he shall die there, where he belongs, unchanged in his belief in the way of life he had fought for.

His brother Jim, unfit for war, had stayed at home and profited by the changing times, taking advantage of his chances with the rising merchants and industrialists. Alienated, hostile, secretly hoping that Ned may die, he watches him go, a breathing reproach, supported by two women of his family. Miss Gordon makes it quite clear, in this short bitter scene, that Jim is the truly defeated man, the lost soul who thinks nothing is worth fighting for, who sets himself to survive and profit meanly by whatever occasion offers him.

This form of opportunism is sometimes at present called "interpreting history correctly"—that is, having the foresight to get on the bandwagon and make the most of the parade. With such shabbiness Miss Gordon has nothing to do. Her story is a legend in praise of heroes, of those who fought well and lost their battle, and their lives. It seems fresh and timely at this moment when we have before our eyes the spectacle of a death-dedicated people holding out in a struggle against overwhelming odds. Of all human impulses, that of heroism changes least in its character and shape, from one epoch to another. He is forever the same, then and forever unanswerable, the man who throws his life away as if he hated living, in defense of the one thing, whatever it may be, that he cares to live for. Causes change perpetually, die, go out of fashion, are superseded according to shifting political schemes, economics, religions, but the men ready to die for them are reborn again and again, always the same men.

Miss Gordon's heart is fixed on the memory of those men who died in a single, superbly fought lost cause, in nothing diminished for being lost, and this devotion has focused her feelings and imagination to a point of fire. She states clearly in every line of her story her mystical faith that what a man lives by, he must if the time comes, die for; to live beyond or to acknowledge defeat is to die twice, and shamefully. The motive of this faith is the pride of Lucifer, and Miss Gordon makes no pretense, either for herself or for her characters, to the maudlin virtue of humility in questions of principle.

All-seeing as an ancient chronicler, she has created a panorama of a society engaged in battle for its life. The author moves about, a disembodied spectator timing her presence expertly, over her familiar territory, Kentucky, Georgia, Tennessee, Mississippi. Time, 1860 to 1864, dates which are, after 1776, the most portentous in the history of this country. Having chosen to observe from all points of view, rather than to stand on a knoll above the battle and watch a set procession of events through a field glass, she makes her scenes move rapidly from Federal lines to Confederate, from hospitals to prisons, to the plantations; the effect could easily have become diffuse without firm handling, and the central inalterable sympathies of the chronicler herself. She might have done the neat conventional thing, and told her story through the adventures of her unlucky young pair of lovers, Lucy Churchill and her cousin, Rives Allard. But they take their proper places in the midst of a tragedy of which their own tragedy is only a part. I know of nothing more humanly touching and immediate than the story of the brief, broken marriage of Rives and Lucy; but the book is not theirs, nor was it meant to be. Rives goes to die as a scout for Nathan Bedford Forrest, that unaccountable genius of war, who remained a mystery and a figure of legend even to his own soldiers, those who knew him best. There is no accounting for Forrest and Miss Gordon does not attempt the impossible. He remains what he was, a hero and a genius.

The Allard family is a center, or rather, a point of departure and return: in the beginning they are clearly seen, alive, each one a human being with his individual destiny, which gradually is merged with the destiny of his time and place. Their ends are symbolically exact: the old man lapses into the escape of imbecility, the old mother into perpetual blind grief, Rives into death in battle, Jim into moral dry rot, Lucy into numbness. In the meantime, we have seen them as they were born to be, busy with the full rich occupations of family life, the work of the plantation, the unpretentious gayety. Life for the Kentucky planters was never so grand as it was in Virginia and Louisiana, or even in Mississippi, with its slightly parvenu manners, if one takes Mr. Stark Young's account at face value. The Kentucky planters were down-to-earth men, and the most tenderly bred women were not above taking a hand in the cookery. They much more resembled Madame Washington than they did Mr. Young's jewelry-conscious belles. This tone is here, properly; it pervades the book like a fresh aroma of green woods and plowed fields.

This seems to me in a great many ways a better book than *Penhally* or *Aleck Maury, Sportsman*, Miss Gordon's other two novels. The good firm style, at once homely, rhythmical and distinguished, is in all three of them, but at its best, so far, in *None Shall Look Back*. It is true I know her story by heart, but I have never heard it told better. The effect is of brilliant, instant life; there is a clear daylight over a landscape I need not close my eyes to see, peopled with figures I know well. I have always known the end, as I know the end of so many tales of love, and heroism, and death. In this retelling, it all happened only yesterday. Those men on the field are not buried yet, those women have just put on their mourning.

✍ The First American Saint

New York Herald Tribune Books, December 12, 1937, p. 2.

Review of *The Life of Saint Rose*, by Marian Storm (Santa Fe: Writers' Editions, 1937).

When the subtle doctors, trying to surprise her secret from her, ambushed her with oblique questions, she answered as exactly as she could. "But in what form, daughter, do you perceive the divinity that thus caresses you and makes you one with him?"

"It is a light," said Saint Rose, "without shape or measure. A glowing that increases. It is incomprehensible, yet comprehending all. It is clear and steady, distant and yet within me . . . as a substance I do not perceive it at all. Indeed, what I perceive is the effect alone. If I were to try forever, father, could I explain discarnate love?"

And the priests, who had been observing and questioning the girl for a great while, assured her worried mother that her daughter was "going forward on a safe road."

Miss Storm has wisely concluded to take their word for it, and has trusted the record set down by the saint's contemporaries. Saints create themselves as works of art; their lives are among the most mysterious of all manifestations of genius. As in all great works of art, there are terrible and even monstrous elements in the beauty of these lives. Churchmen, of the devoted and practical kind who keep the organization intact and functioning as it should, fear them and fight them, and end by absorbing and canonizing them. There is no other way of defeating them. Miss Storm has devoted attention, sympathy, scholarship and good common sense to the superb example of sainthood that was the life of Saint Rose. She was born Flores, christened Isabel, later called Rose, in the city of Lima, Peru, in May, 1586, and died there, in a long, mystically self-induced agony, on August 24, 1617. Her historical priorities are three: she is the first American saint, the only American woman saint and the only saint born in America. She seemed conscious of her destiny in these things, for she offered herself as the victim for the expiation of the sins of all America, and its advocate modelling her life and penances upon those of the great St. Catherine of Siena at first, until she had grown to that stature where she might leave off the role of disciple.

Her parents were poor, but of the respectable class in the oh, so Spanish meaning of that phrase, "gente decente" and they were good Catholics and loving if somewhat excitable parents, especially her mother, and it seemed quite fitting that having a daughter of exceptional beauty, they would make a fine marriage for her and so consolidate the position of the family in good society. She was a joyous saint, who played the guitar and sang duets with a wren, a flower gardener who had miraculous success with her blooms, a needle woman who helped support her family. (This reminds me of St. Joan's boast to her judges, "in the matter of needle and thread I fear no woman in Rouen.") She did the roughest and most menial work of her household, and kept the fine beauty of her hands. She wished to go into a convent, but her parents forbade her, so she built a little hermitage for herself in the family garden, and it still stands, such a good solid worker she was. For years, in the bosom of her mystified and horribly annoyed family she practiced such methodical self-torture as raises the hair even to read about.

When the important offer of a good marriage came on in due course, her mother and father and even her brothers joined heartily to beat her into submission. But she withstood them and won. "Jesus a thousand times," cried her poor mother, "a dozen normal children and then along comes this one."

She had a habit of stooping to straighten twigs, or other objects which had fallen cruciform, for fear that some careless foot might tread upon the shape of the cross. Her brother Fernando, walking with her, would give her the most crushing worldly rebuke possible, no doubt glancing around fearfully to see who observed them. "You will make fools of us both—come on," he told her. He was her favorite brother, and a good sixteenth century Spanish boy, who thought of nothing but appearances.

Saint Rose was a Catharist, as all the self-mortifying saints were. She believed that the flesh was of the devil, and the spirit was of God. She was the Bride of Christ, and he gave her a gold ring, and her whole life was a marriage feast to which the flesh was not invited. As Miss Storm points out, psychology was not discovered yesterday, and the men who examined the experiences of Saint Rose were by no means unworldly, but deeply instructed in the ways of human nature, and they had the proper fear and distrust of female nature, which is corrupt to the marrow. They were as keenly on the lookout for sexual aberrations and for perverted instincts as any Freudian, but they were more adroit in beating about the bush for it was above all things necessary not to give scandal. They found her a first rank mystic, and so pronounced her, and about seventy years after her death, formally proclaimed her a saint.

✍ Lovely Evocative Photographs

New York Herald Tribune Books, March 8, 1942, p. 4.

Review of *New Orleans and Its Living Past*, photographs by Clarence John Laughlin, text by David L. Cohn (Boston: Houghton Mifflin Company, 1941).

This is a quite handsome book, well bound with good type, clear wide margins, the photographs reproduced extremely well on good heavy paper. There are sixty-two photographs and thirty pages of text.

It is a romantic enterprise, as if two men, friendly toward each other, were infatuated with the same woman without jealousy, and had collaborated in making the most flattering portrait possible of her. Mr. Cohn admits the truth cheerfully: Mr. Laughlin's camera "has succeeded where words fail." Mr. Cohn's words by no means fail altogether. His rapid sketch of the early history of New Orleans is very lively and hits all the familiar high spots, well chosen to show the gay colors and the individual features of the city: the French Opera, the pirates, the gentlemen fighting duels over ladies of easy virtue, the Casket Girl, the Quadroon Balls, the food, the slave blocks set up near the entrances of the great hotels, the yellow fever, John Law's Mississippi Bubble, all are here, with insistence on the mean origins of the early settlers and a good slap at Southern pride in family history as he goes.

We have read it all before many times—in fact, it is about all we can find to read about New Orleans. Savory bits of local gossip and old scandals are heaped together profusely like a haul of fish on the levee. The effect is marred somewhat by the tone of snobbishness and rudeness toward the absurd uninitiated visitor who comes, at the urgent invitation of the Chamber of Commerce, innocently to spend his money and gawk at all the wrong things, eating beefsteak and potatoes when he could have gumbo and oysters Rockefeller. Gumbo is certainly something not to be missed, and I doubt if even the most unenlightened tourist manages to miss it. As for oysters Rockefeller, the dish is superb, but the name is all wrong. A sign of the times and a bad sign. But Mr. Cohn dashes on, with the eagerness and enthusiasm of the new broom, sweeping all before him.

At the risk of being elected to the I-Knew-It-When club, I venture timidly to remember New Orleans when it seemed to rain all the time and I woke up in the morning to the sound of the breakfast coffee being ground, and the shouts of Black Mammies clothed in faded flowered dresses, white aprons and bandanas, who were peddling all sorts of things to eat; but I remember only fish, plantains, herbs and pralines. They were not out to present a picturesque appearance under the auspices of the local tourist bureau, they were wearing what they were used to wearing, and they were selling their vittles in dead earnest, hoping to make an honest living strictly under their own power. At that time, the Vieux Carré was a uniform soot-

color perhaps because most of those who lived there could not afford
a coat of paint, and those who could did not think it necessary. Visitors often remark on the scarcity of fresh paint in the South. The
reason is, or was, that the money always simply gave out before we
could get round to fresh paint. It was the unattainable luxury. Well,
I yield to no one in my love of improvement; I am constitutionally
unable to let anything, even a rented flat, remain as it is. But just the
same I found New Orleans a saddish place to revisit after so many
long years.

It was pleasant to see the Vieux Carré being shored up and cleaned
up and treasured as it deserves to be, but I felt that the motives were
dubious, and the effect had a little too much of stage property in it—
all façade. The sweet familiar smells were there, boiling molasses
and brown sugar, roasting pecans and dried vetiver, and the strange
heart-thrilling whiff of tropical flowers mingled with the cool odor of
mold from old patios. All of these were there, mingled with another,
the stink of political corruption which hangs nose high in air and
seems to exude like a rancid sweat from the very walls. The organized
Bohemia is perhaps the dullest and most pretentious in America. I
say this with reserve, not having seen all the Bohemias. All political
and social activity seemed to be in the grip of those who wielded
alternately the battle ax and the cold chisel. There was a shameless
cynicism in the administering of public affairs calculated to chill the
blood. Mr. Cohn's words fail, then, on the side of frivolity and love of
the surface aspect of things, and he has fallen into the common error
of putting on airs about his special knowledge, which is not so very
special after all, and of looking down his nose at the less privileged
visitor.

The photographs are quite another matter. They are full of melancholy light and shade, as New Orleans is, at any time of year, any
hour of the day. The lenses are trained frankly on the romantic detail,
the picturesque long shot. The very texture of the building materials,
the pattern of the lacy iron work, the harmonious relation between a
wall, a fountain, and a tree, are shown as they appear really to any one
who loves them. For me the book is a wonderful personal possession,

because it gives the best view I ever saw of the lower Pontalba on St. Ann Street, seen through Jackson Square. I lived once on the top floor of the lower Pontalba, right-hand corner, and Jackson Square was to me then and is still one of the mysteriously enchanting places of the world. My very favorite camphor tree is in this picture. The Cabildo never looked more like itself than in its new photograph. I miss the French market, but it isn't so pretty since it was cleaned up and inclosed. The study of St. Louis Cathedral, with its cross resting against a white cloud and the great ram's head in the near foreground looming over the left-hand tower, is superb. St. Louis's is one of the busiest places in town. I have seen going on there at once a wedding, a funeral and a christening party, with a crowd of personally conducted tourists taking it all in, milling around and getting underfoot, rather, but accepted as a part of life, as, indeed, they had the right to be.

Only the most beautiful and touching things are in these photographs, and I think properly so, because they are vanishing little by little, by outright demolition, or by restoration not always carried on in the light of their true history, and such a record as this may one day be all that remains of them. It is true that brave and honest efforts are being made by a number of citizens to rescue the best of their city from the clutches of commercial and political forces, but they seem to be losing rather steadily.

This is a very evocative book. It reminds one who loved New Orleans of all that was worth keeping there, and how little of it has been kept. But New Orleans, even now, just the place itself—the colors and sounds, the heavy air, the heat, the rain, the smells, the shapes of some things—is lovely, and Mr. Laughlin has seen this particular reality in its true light and without once cocking a superior snoot at any one.

✍ The Sparrow Revolution

Nation, vol. 154, no. 12 (March 21, 1942), p. 343.

Review of *The Pink Egg*, by Polly Boyden (Truro, Mass.: Pamet Press, 1942).

This is a fable about the downtrodden, underprivileged sparrows who make a revolution and throw all the robins and other handsomer, luckier, and more talented birds out of the orchard where they live, and some of the very nicest robins turn in and help them. As one of the singing birds says, wistfully: "But all you sparrows are so much closer to the future than we other birds; so you must show us how to get there because we do not want to lose our way."

Why choose sparrows out of all the bird world to represent the human downtrodden and underprivileged? They are fairly dull-looking little birds who do not sing; they are the most gluttonous of small birds except the bluejay, so lecherous they have become the symbol of human incontinence, and so quarrelsome there is no getting on with them at all. Any bird can tell you. If you want to get down on sparrows just watch them descend on a feeding station where robins and wrens and mocking birds and all sorts of sweet singing creatures are sharing their food in peace. Will the sparrows allow this to go on? No, they scatter the others with blows and curses and then fight among themselves as they lick the platter clean. Only the bluejay can beat them at this game, and only because he is bigger and has a tougher beak. Ounce for ounce, the sparrow is meaner than a bluejay. He simply hasn't got the heft.

If the future of the bird world is really with the sparrows, it is a grim prospect. It is significant, too, that the sparrows were able to enlist almost the whole bird race in an unselfish labor to further the good of—you've guessed it, the sparrows. They say the campaign will be for the improvement of all, but nothing in their conduct leads you to believe this. They lack almost everything it takes to create a good world, they are as noisy and selfish and dull as some people, really; but what is good for sparrows, they say, will be plenty good enough for other birds: they'll take it and like it, or they'll have to go, that's all. They will be spared to work, however, until they have finished helping the sparrows build a world in which nothing a sparrow cannot appreciate will be permitted to exist.

St. Francis doped the birds, preaching to them that way, says one debunking sparrow. But if birds are what this book makes them out to be, it is possible that the birds doped poor St. Francis. At any rate, if they were sparrows, he wasted his breath talking to them. They'll never learn by that method.

The symbol of the lighthouse in this story interests me because it illustrates the danger of turning the world over to the sparrows. This lighthouse stands on an island, the only spot hospitable to sparrows; in the jacket note it is identified as danger and desire. Left to myself I might have thought it stood for Truth or the Light of Reason or Morality. Whatever it may mean, there is something sinister in the attitude of the sparrows toward this lighthouse. It is the creation of human beings, who collectively seem to mean, to the birds, a higher power which distributes its favors on a mysterious plan: the island is free to any bird who can reach it, and it is meant to be a place of shelter and peace. What is the meaning of the lighthouse? the birds ask among themselves. A sparrow remarks that they don't know yet what it means, but they will look into the question later, and there is a hint that once the birds find their way to the island, they will put out the light, since they will not need it any more.

Now if the lighthouse really signifies danger and desire, those birds are very silly to think they can abolish it. And if it should mean guidance, for example, and was put there for the convenience and safety of birds, their plan to put it out when they no longer need it seems to me shortsighted and selfish to the last degree. There will always be birds in the infinite future trying to find their way to the island.

Well, these birds build fires and wear orange felt hats and wield apple axes and carry away their wounded on stretchers, and if the author is not really talking about birds, I am. I say it is a grim little slander on the birds, and on that part of the human race typified by the sparrows. I don't think the working people, the proletariat as they used to be called, are at all like sparrows, and I think the choice of such a comparison is not very tactful to say the least.

It is odd, also, to find another fallacy: the intelligent, poetic, inspired, and heroic birds in the feathered revolutionary movement are nearly all renegades from the upper classes who sacrifice their fortunes and devote their talents to their less fortunate brethren. I don't agree with this thesis. Those birds from the upper classes haven't been half as important as they like to believe. I think most of them have had a good time and got more than they gave. The really heavy job has been done by the working people.

As for these birds with their unpleasantly human ways, I am reminded irresistibly of the beachcomber's fable about the man who tried to make the mice in his house wear little wool hats during the cold weather. He wasn't any more successful than Miss Boyden trying to make her birds wear waistcoats, but he was a great deal funnier.

✍ Mexico's Thirty Long Years of Revolution

New York Herald Tribune Books, May 30, 1943, pp. 1–2.

Review of *The Wind That Swept Mexico*, by Anita Brenner
(New York: Harper and Brothers, 1943).

In Cuernavaca there is a pavement with the celebrated commemorative motto, "It is more honorable to die standing than to live kneeling." The great beauty of this saying, the reason no doubt why it rings with such confident reassurance in the mind, is that the Mexican revolutionists always knew it was true and acted upon it long before any one thought of making the phrase. They have not only died standing, but attacking, weapons in hand, their spiritual boots on. I say spiritual boots because many of them in fact were barefooted. Mexico is comparatively a small country, yet by conservative esti-

mate a million men have died for this cause: that is to say, for the
most primary and rudimentary things of life for a man, a scrap of land
to grow his food, and official legal recognition of his mere humanity
by government and society. Mexico is potentially a vastly rich country, so seven-tenths, perhaps, of her enemies have come from without; the other three-tenths, as happens in all countries, we know
more clearly than ever now, are among her own people. For more
than thirty long, bitter years the Mexican revolutionists have fought
for the minimum of human rights against a mostly ungodly united
force consisting of their own proto-Quislings, the Church, the oil and
metal-mining companies of the United States and Great Britain, the
trading interests of Germany and the stubborn reactionary hold of
Spanish influence. There were besides the internal quarrels between
the various schools of revolution, the personal rivalries, individual
struggles for mere power, all the most dreary and average history of
human weakness and failure. Yet for all of this the Mexican revolutionists have made a good showing; they exhibited high qualities of
tenaciousness, personal courage, incorrigible love of country, a fixed
determination not to live kneeling, besides a gradually developing
sense of method, of political strategy, and a pretty fair understanding of just what they were up against in a world sense. The whole
story of the relations of that country with the United States alone
is ugly, grim, bitter beyond words, and so scandalous I suppose the
whole truth, or even the greater part of the simple facts, can never
be published: it might blow the roof off this continent.

Keeping these things well in mind, Miss Brenner has written a
rather light sketch of the whole period, hitting the high spots only
but choosing the spots so tactfully that the plot is never lost; and
though I have known the story, and for many years, so well it is possible I fill in the gaps as I go, yet I like to feel that the reader who
knows little can find here a clear statement, a logical exposition, that
will serve safely as a starting point if he wishes to pursue this history
further. The facts are straight so far as they go, the deep, underlying
motives of the whole restless and aspiring period are understood and
explained, but I think Miss Brenner yields again to her old temptation

to give too pretty and simple a picture—for, mind you, this terrible little story she tells is a mere bedtime lullaby beside the reality—and in general, to treat individual villains, whom she really knows to be such, too gently. A few scorching lines it seems to me might have been devoted to, for example, Alberto Pani's career as Foreign Minister. I think the deeds of some of the oil companies could have been exposed with somewhat more vigor. The betrayal of Felipe Carillo-Puerto might have been clarified to the great benefit of the story. Yet, within the limitations of space—the story is only 100 pages long— the author has performed prodigies of condensation, and within the more multiple and complicated limitations of the present international political situation, she has perhaps ventured as far as she might and still have her book published at all.

The best thing is, she realizes the importance of easy relations between Mexico and the United States just now, and the dangers, too; for, as she says frankly, this being the point of the book, that as the diplomatic and other understandings between the United States and the Mexican governments grow amiable, the Mexican people grow uneasy for their own prospects of freedom; and they may well do so, for Lavals and Pétains do not grow only in France. The Mexican people have been handed over to the invaders by their own leaders before, and they are not so childish as to think it cannot happen again. Invasion takes many forms, and they have experienced most of them.

Mr. Leighton's collection of pictures is distinguished, realistic; with extracts from Miss Brenner's texts, they could stand as a book by themselves. . . . They tell the story all over again and in some ways more boldly, of a whole race disinherited in its own country and fighting against desperate odds. Besides being superior photography, chosen with a fine sense of form and progression, these pictures lack entirely the slickness, the made-to-order look, of too much of the photography in this present war, which gives the impression that the man with the camera has instructions to shoot from only certain angles and no others: "A little," wrote a friend not long ago, "as if this war were something being produced by M.G.M." Happily, these Mexican pictures were made before that period set in. They have a

wonderfully casual air; the man with the camera took what he saw
before him, whatever it happened to be, not thinking, apparently,
whether it would be good propaganda or not. . . . It turns out that
he made the most convincing, most moving kind of straight narrative; and, oh, the faces. . . . It seems to me one need not be partisan;
one need only to be human in the most average way, not to see what
was bound to happen, comparing, let's say, just the face of Zapata (in
Tina Modotti's masterly working out of an old negative) with that of
Archbishop Pascual Diaz; or of Hearst with that of Obregon, taken
when his shattered arm was healing, and not to be able to know at
once which side one is on, now and forever. . . .

✍ They Lived with the Enemy in the House

New York Herald Tribune Weekly Book Review, March 4, 1945, p. 1.

Review of *Apartment in Athens,* by Glenway Wescott (New York:
Harper and Brothers, 1945).

Since this short history of what "happened" to a Greek family named
"Helianos" is as current in its subject matter as the headline in this
morning's newspaper, the important thing to know about *Apartment
in Athens* is that it is first of all a work of honest, unembarrassed good
literature. It is useful in the sense that no good work of art can ever be
anything but useful, and timely because it can never come too early or
too late. It is a story of the shapeless, immoderate miseries and confusions brought by the Germans upon this world for the third time
within the memory of living men; it is even "propaganda" against
this Germanic savagery, if you like, and if you would call Goya's *Dis-
asters of War* by such a name. Mr. Wescott is said to have remarked
that he wrote the book "to show how bad the Germans are"—but he
has gone much further than that. Surely nobody need tell us at this
time of day how bad the Germans are: they themselves first told us

years ago; and then for years they have demonstrated their meaning precisely. Mr. Wescott has done something much more valuable than that: he has exposed and anatomized that streak of Germanism in the rest of us which made possible the Germany we know today. He does not indulge in any such generalization as this, but takes full advantage of the blessed craft of fiction, which calls for compression, limitation, severe choice of incident and a minute attention to those particular traits of character in the individual human being in a given locality and time. It is not his business to report corpses by the ton, destruction by the cityful, famine by thousands of square miles, losses on bombing missions by so much material. His scene is Greece; Athens; a poor four-room flat in a dingy street; his story the long painful education of Mr. and Mrs. Helianos in the true nature of evil, not only in their barbarous guest, but in themselves; and at last the true meaning of courage, a knowledge delayed so late it was almost useless, but not quite.

When the German captain chose their poor little flat for his quarters because it was convenient to his place of work, and began his highly instructed course of humiliation and terror in the household, Mr. and Mrs. Helianos were already experienced in defeat. Comfortable members of the upper middle class, the husband a mild-mannered middle-aged publisher with a civilized, poetic erudition, they had lost their first and best loved son at the battle of Mount Olympus; had been driven out of their house into a starveling neighborhood; had watched their small son and daughter dwindle with famine, the boy's brilliant mind gone savage and oblique, the girl stunned into half-wittedness by the sight of violence.

Mrs. Helianos has reason to believe that her brother has treasonable dealings with the Germans. She longs not to believe it, then wishes to believe it because by such means his life is saved; then tries to excuse him; then secretly hopes he is dead because by her logic the disgrace would be softened, she would be free to forget him. Mr. Helianos comes of a bolder family, his male cousins are off in the mountains still fighting and doing underground work. He had always deplored in his rational, philosophic way, their reckless bravery while admiring their spirit. Still it seems to him at first that intelligent ruse, strategy, patience, a certain appearance of bending to the yoke while maintaining mental reservations, must in the long run overcome what he considers as mere raw blind force.

It is to be seen that even before the German captain came upon them they had set their feet in the longest and bitterest way. They become slaves in their own apartment to a pompous minor god with nasty personal habits and an epileptic instability of temper, the range of whose virtuosity in mean cruelties is endless. Helianos, still "trying to understand the Germans in general by this officer," and comparing notes with his Greek fellow sufferers, begins to grasp little by little that there was nothing unpremeditated in German behavior anywhere. They practised torture with "various tricks that were like surgery gone wrong, with little up-to-date mechanical contraptions."

Still, Helianos argues with himself and with his wife, whose feelings are deep, truly maternal and untinged with what, in spite of her loyal, impatient love, she considers her husband's male sophistries. He argues that they are better off than the people of Crete, where mere massacre had been carried out with the most acute disciplines and formalities. They are lucky in their officer—he belongs to the quarter-masters corps, not the ranks of killers and torturers. He did desk work and had intellectual interests. There is, he confesses weakly, even a certain charm about the fellow when he is not annoyed. Their chances for survival are more than fair.

It all comes to nothing in the deep places of their beings where they truly live and cannot avoid self-knowledge. They realize that "their having been able to bear it would be nothing to boast of. They thought of it as . . . a disease all through them, like vermin all over them. That would be their story and they would be ashamed to tell it."

Happily it is not their story. The captain, after a short sharp reign of terror, goes to Germany, has there an experience which shakes him, returns with the look of a haunted man, and becomes suddenly, frighteningly amiable to his prisoners. He draws Helianos into long strange conversations, in which he explains with the exaltation of mania his inhuman creed. He weeps and complains because the war has destroyed his wife and children, on the very soil of Germany the war has come and taken those sacred lives. Helianos listens, the divided, thoughtful, civilized man longing to be just even to his enemy, seeking the truth even from the very teeth of evil. But he cannot in the end, in spite of his own efforts, betray or degrade his spirit any longer. Without knowing, almost as if by a slip of the tongue, almost as if by mere childish credulity, he speaks the few words that open the trap that has been set there for him from the beginning, not purposely by the captain, but by the very nature of the situation.

From there the history of the Helianos family goes to its beautiful, reassuring end. It could be read now simply for what it has to tell us about the enemy, whom we helped to create. It might help us to recognize what it is in ourselves that has given him such power. As a work of literature it might do what no amount of newspaper print can accomplish in touching our hard hearts and stubborn minds. That could well be its purpose for now. But I cannot foresee a time when Helianos's letter to his wife, smuggled from prison, when he was dying under "questioning" and "did not always feel well" might not be read as poetry when happily, happily, its readers may no longer need the instruction it contains.

"I really know nothing about Americans. . . . Only I feel sure that they will be most important again when the war is over. Probably the Russians are ruthless, but the British have too much sense of honor and sentiment for the job that is to be done, and the Americans can influence the British.

"Tell Petros to warn them beyond the sea that it may happen to them, too, before the century is over. Nothing is too difficult for these great mystical, scientific, hard-working, self-denying Germans, possessed of the devil as they are, and despising every one else.

"I do not suppose that the Americans are indifferent to their fate and danger. I think that their worst mistake must be in their hope of getting peace established for all time, as if it were a natural law needing no enforcement, so that they can relax and be frivolous and forget it. When they see that this is not possible then they lose hope altogether. They give it all up as a bad job and yield to their cynicism and fatalism. It is what happened after the other war. . . .

"What on earth do they mean when they speak of peace forever?

Naturally it can only be a little at a time, with good luck, and with an effort and great vigilance and good management, day by day, year after year. Life is like that; everything on earth is like that; have the Americans and the British forgotten? . . .

"When we are sick and we go to see a doctor, do we expect him to promise us immortality?" . . .

✍ This Strange, Old World

New York Times Book Review, August 20, 1950, pp. 5, 17.

Review of *The Secret Game*, by François Boyer, trans. Michael Legat (New York: Harcourt, Brace and Company, 1950); and *The House of Breath*, by William Goyen (New York: Random House, 1950).

The young writers, after an experience of war, maybe four or more years at the crucial point of their youth, seem to share one common feeling of strangeness to the world to which they have returned, for all appear to agree that they have lately been visitors to another planet. They were alien to that planet, and now to this one also. This one is perhaps even more strange than the other. They are wrong, because they have never been away, they have been in this world all the time. What seems so odd is that nothing in their lives before, nor any one they knew—those older persons charged with their education—seems in the least to have prepared them for what they were to find here. So everything comes at once to them as a horrifying shock, a nightmare, and a final disillusion.

These two of a dozen first books by unknown writers I have seen lately interest me because they are the work of two young men, serious beginning artists, of two different levels, maybe, but that remains to be seen. They are alike in fearlessness, and what they have to tell is not disgraceful to them; it is only a disturbing reminder to the rest of us.

The first, François Boyer, is French, and so, of course, he suffers a little in translation; almost everybody does. He was born in 1920 in a small town in the north of France. The note on the publisher's jacket says nothing of his military service, but he has seen the war, enough of it for his purposes.

A 9-year-old girl, Paulette, his protagonist, the bringer of death, the innocent partaker of death, lies beside the road where a long procession of human beings, followed by their animals, are fleeing from death, while the Germans above are swooping down upon them from time to time, dropping a bomb where they hope it will have the most effect.

She has learned to identify individuals by their feet, that is, the shape and color of their wounds: she straggles after her father, whose feet have wounds on them like crushed blackberries, until he is killed. She is seized upon by crazed women looking for their lost children, kissed horribly, called by every girl-name there is, repulsed again, until, leaving her father's body without looking back, she wanders across a field, picks up the dead dog which had a little while before stopped beside her and showed his wounds. She carries him to the edge of a wood beside a stream, and goes on to be taken in as a stray harmless animal might be, by a family of French peasants. The story is of the secret death-bound alliance between her and the younger son of the family, Michel.

The contrivances of Boyer's book are simple and direct, the structure very workmanlike. He uses easily all sorts of the most familiar devices, old and yet as effective as ever if used honorably; mystery and suspense, interplay of motive between consistent and therefore predictable characters, and a linking of episode with episode in a straight progression of time. By these means he manages to give a daylight air to a story of darkness, of two children playing a doomed game with the only reality they know—death.

Boyer has made a special study of scenario writing at the Institut des Hautes Etudes Cinématographiques, in Paris, a sort of institution unknown here, the lack of which accounts in part for the difference between the best French films and the best American product. One may very easily see an admirable motion picture in this book; the writer is supposed to have drawn rather heavily upon his knowledge of screen requirements. Maybe, but this is most certainly a novel in the most traditional style, and of the kind that in the past quarter-century has often been referred to, pejoratively, as "well made."

The Secret Game is an interesting, honest, small work; not perfect, not in the least a cameo, done objectively, at arm's length. No one speaks or acts except the characters. The author is nowhere visible, though he could be the voice of the narrator, a little dry and bitter, following the action of the film; but the shadows on the screen are full of mysterious feeling, they are not puppets but shadows cast by the living.

William Goyen's first book, *The House Of Breath*, is not a well-made novel, indeed it is not a novel at all but a sustained evocation of the past, a long search for place and identity, and the meaning of an intense personal experience; an attempt to cleanse the heart of its mysterious burden of guilt, to build with words, breath-made substance, a bridge over the gulf between two disassociated experiences.

Mr. Goyen is not yet 30, and spent four-and-one-half years in the Navy during the war. He was born in a small town in East Texas, which he calls Charity, and that is the scene of his story. It is on one plane a typical chronicle which in our country seems only to come from the family-haunted, family-cursed South, that of the decayed house falling about its apathetic, obsessed inmates, the land rotting away unused in its own richness, the young ignorant children growing up, living for the day when they can pack their suitcases and head for life, opportunity, in the nearest big town. The evil has been progressive: I saw it begin in my generation, and, judging by this latest history, the walls that then were leaning are now rotted into the earth.

Many of these lost families cling to their fading legend of good birth, former wealth. There remain in their speech echoes of a richer language than that of the present; in their feelings a jealous exclusiveness in family love, in habits and ways no matter how slatternly and deathly they have become. It is only six or seven generations, sometimes fewer, since the bold, proud stubborn ancestors of these people went in to break wildernesses literally with their own bodies.

It is as if the effort had not only broken them—some of them, these we are talking about—but their descendants, and it has taken all this time for a new kind of energy and will to sprout once more among them. Now and again up from the mould one child will rise and go, and seek to become, feeling himself a Judas and a deserter, never to be forgiven, never to escape from the bitter love and reproach of those he left.

This is the background, or rather, the scene, the overwhelming present, of this book in St. Augustine's sense: "Thus my childhood, which now is not, is in time past, which now is not, but now when I recall its image and tell of it, I behold it in the present, because it is [present] in my memory."

Everything is present, everything is articulate, nothing is impersonal: the history is intimate, the symbols all sexual. The river has a voice, it tells its own story, it helps the returned exile to remember part of his own. The wind has a hundred voices, it blows "out a long tale in the shutter," sings down chimneys and old stove pipes. The cistern wheel has a voice, and the well itself; the cellar has a voice; and these voices have the tone of those dead or vanished beings who cling to the familiar places like spirits who reject both heaven and hell and have returned to their small sad limbo. For the voices speaking out of the wells and on the wind tell such old sad stories of love, fertility, richness, all the glory of the world, gone astray, wasted, lost; terrible stories of the stuff of life, the capacity for love, the fertility of women, the virile force of men, all misused, misunderstood, perverted and rotting in its own juices. Yet by the very power of the bewitched memory which dwells upon them with love, sometimes with an excessive tenderness almost as obsessed as that of the anguished, deserted women, there is revealed, very darkly and deep down, a strangely unviolated center of pure being, where life might very well spring again.

Mr. Goyen has not availed himself of any of the precautions against self-revelation that is so useful in the objective method. Here are the most extravagant feelings, the most absurd recklessness of revealment, at times there is real danger of the fatal drop into over-pathos, over-saying: a boyish tearfulness over some very dubious attachments and admirations. But then, that belongs to childish life, that time of exorbitant experience which pushes at the boundaries of speech and beyond, until "it all ends, in wordlessness, and my tears."

To balance this fault, the writing as a whole is disciplined on a high plane, and there are long passages of the best writing, the fullest and richest and most expressive, that I have read in a very long time—complex in form, and beautifully organized, shapely as a good tree, as alive and as substantial.

✍ A Quaker Who "Had a Splendid Time of It"

New York Herald Tribune Book Review, September 24, 1950, p. 6.

Review of *Philadelphia Quaker: The Letters of Hannah Whitall Smith*, ed. Logan Pearsall Smith (New York: Harcourt, Brace and Company, 1950).

In the twenties and maybe before, Logan Pearsall Smith was the adored Old Maestro to the oddest assortment of young men who wrote. I remember one who wrote the most grinding little bores of books in the style of "He grabbed her bare thigh and squeezed hard, it felt like a dead fish," school, who told me he modeled his prose rhythms on the noise of a planing mill within earshot while he was writing. Another imitated verbally the sound effects of a jazz band in full swing. Still another—no, there were too many, and they all admired Logan Pearsall Smith extravagantly. Naturally this threw me off, and I avoided Logan Pearsall Smith as others do the Devil. Later when these young writing men had disappeared and the excitement had died down about the Maestro, I read his memoirs, *Unforgotten Years*; this led to *Trivia* and other works, and so to Robert Gaythorne-Hardy's *Recollections* of his strange friend and malevolent benefactor; all books to be read by any one interested in that particular period in English literature and its main figures, for that curious gifted personality touched almost every one and everything at one point of his experience or another.

After the death in 1911 of his mother, who had been a celebrated Quaker preacher and writer of religious books, Smith discovered also that she was "a most remarkable and brilliant letter-writer," and he selected these letters which now appear. I believe his judgment was right. They glow with the utmost vitality and sincerity of feeling, the most independent powers of observation and remark, and the most gay, warm good humor. They cover the period between her fifteenth and her seventy-ninth, and last, year, and from the beginning they have that tone of informal good talk which is the secret of first rate letter writers.

With her force of character and religious fervor, she was in great danger: she might have become a canting bore or a dangerous fanatic. But that clear appraising eye that she could turn on others she could also turn upon herself, and her most secret motives. In her earlier days, she was considered heretical because she did not believe in eternal punishment for sinners; she thought God incapable of such injustice. In the end, she came to the charming conclusion, prompted by her own human affections, that God simply meant for people to live as good human beings behaving well to each other in this mortal condition, and in this state of grace she maintained herself to the end.

Meantime, she renounced the world as a young girl, and day-dreamed that "all of a sudden, in some unaccountable way I should get perfectly good, just like Madame Guyon," but also she was going to be such a marvelous preacher her hearers would be almost ready to fall down and worship her. By the time this did in fact come nearly true, she had got dreams well separated from realities. Twice afterward she renewed it with fresh heart and energy: once in middle age when she went to begin with her husband a new phase of their religious career in England, and again in real old age when she found herself joyously made guardian of her two Catholic granddaughters.

She had great beauty, which surely never did her any harm, though she seems to have ignored its existence and its effect on others.

She was a natural born mother who just the same "liked men, but not husbands," as a friend explained; her deep distrust of marriage as a medium of human happiness tended to be confirmed as time went on: and of her seven adored children, four died, at birth or in earliest infancy or in youth; her erratic, gifted, overstrung husband committed some indiscretions not altogether unconnected with the sexual taboos of the time, and the ensuing scandal crushed him and spoiled his life, though not his wife's—she lived in this world as a passing stranger, and even good reputation might sometimes be looked upon as a worldly vanity. The things of this world were real enough, sometimes pleasant enough, but nothing to set one's heart upon.

Based solidly on material wealth and good social position, evangelical religion, with its anti-intellectual, anti-esthetic, reforming, pietistic, utterly middle class genteel point of view, was extraordinarily in favor among a large number of the British nobility and gentry. So her religious work carried her much into titled society and her family relations much into the company of as dedicated a lot of esthetes as England could afford. There was of course her son Logan, a man of letters if ever there was one; her daughter Alys married Bertrand Russell; her daughter Mary married Bernard Berenson; her granddaughter Ray married a Strachey; Roger Fry, a Quaker who held the most astounding views on painting, was Logan's favorite authority on the subject; William James, Madame Blavatsky, Lord Tennyson, eighty-three, came and went through her receptive yet resistant consciousness: she loved to watch people's minds at work; it did not after all so much matter what they thought.

In her youth she had not got along with Walt Whitman; he had taken her for a saint, which was his mistake; but it ruined any possibility of understanding between them. Oscar Wilde, however, on two far separated occasions, had spoken to her deepest spiritual perceptions: "One of my greatest openings into the mystery of religion came from something I heard him say in Philadelphia, dressed in shorts with a big sunflower in his buttonhole. He said, 'You can conquer a city by force, but you can only conquer the art of that city by submission to its rules.' " And again, with her son Logan, then aged seventeen, she remembered part of another lecture: "To the true artist there is no time but the artistic moment; and no land but the land of beauty." She remarked: "He does say now and then a fine thing about art, just about what I would say about religion."

She became a world traveler and for years her letters are dated from all sorts of unlikely places: she enjoys everything, and looks at it with the cheerful detached eye of one who need not linger, need not claim anything, need not look back. Her children are nostalgic when she gives up their old house where they were brought up, and moves to a flat. Not she; that was then, and now is now, one lives always with God in the present moment. The present moment is never dull, we may be sure. She goes to the races, to a stag-chase, to the theater; she pursues the impenetrable mysteries of taste in painting and music; she wonders at her daughters' choice of husbands; she sees that her son Logan has turned out about as she prophesied—not badly, on the whole—and everything she says has the freshness of the innocent eye and mind, innocent, not simple; the honest realism of a mind deeply capable of love but not of sentimentality; a sound tough streak of sternness, but not coldness; great patience, but nobody's martyr or dupe. The only times she suffered in relative silence, until her final rebellion, were on the awful recurring August vacations of her American years when her children dragged her on the most bone-crushing expeditions in the wilds; her accounts of these times are among the gayest of all her letters. She wouldn't have missed them for anything.

You close this book with that final feeling about her: surely no one liked the mere state of living better than she did; she had a splendid time of it. She wished at the end, she said, to be whisked off astride the tail of a comet. Nothing could have been more suitable to her style.

✍ A Most Lively Genius

New York Times Book Review, November 18, 1951, pp. 5, 52.

Review of *Short Novels of Colette*, with an introduction by
Glenway Wescott (New York: Dial Press, 1951).

The important thing to read in this collection is Glenway Wescott's introduction. It is a labor of love, affectionate but unblinded; a deserved tribute to a most lively genius, full of Mr. Wescott's wry judgments—all well seated in a long knowledge of all the works, in French—possibly the only language that can ever really contain them—and a true introduction. This long study, or meditation, on the life and writings of Colette does his dear author the justice to tell the new reader who is depending on translations that these short novels, for all their varying brilliancy, are not her best work.

He re-tells from her own autobiographical writings, and with more reserve than she, the highlights of that long, difficult, complicated life of hers, much more absorbing, much deeper and more truthful, than any of her fictions. He relates this life, headlong, willful, full of gaiety and suffering, "almost scandalous," as he says, yet strangely disciplined and austere in sum, to her work; in the end she could absorb, survive, re-see and re-make almost everything. To an astonishing degree she could use her experience as an artist and yet not lose her memory of what it cost her as a living, growing human being; so that her later writings, especially about her disastrous, perverse first marriage, have a strange daylight, morning freshness on them that her earlier work did not have.

It was hardly fair to American readers to have kept Colette from them for so long; nor fair to Colette, either, who should have been the fashion here at least twenty-five years ago—when we think how her lessers were being brought in all that time with fanfares, from every direction. In France she has been known and loved and read from the beginning, and though one always heard of her as "a light writer," that was no term of disrespect—quite the contrary. The French above all know how much strength and discipline and even sheer genius it takes to write lightly of serious things; they never called her frivolous, far from it.

Yet there was always that tone of particular indulgence, reserved for gifted women who make no pretentions and know how to keep their place in the arts: a modest second-best, no matter how good, to the next ranking male, Wescott, mentioning that both Proust and Gide wrote her letters of praise, says, flatly: "For, now that the inditers are both dead and gone, Colette is the greatest living French fiction writer."

I agree to this extent: that she is the greatest living French writer of fiction; and that she was while Gide and Proust still lived; that these two preposterously afflicted self-adoring, frankly career-geniuses certainly got in Colette's light; they certainly diminished her standing, though not her own kind of genius. She lived in the same world, more or less in the same time—without their money or their leisure. Where they could choose their occasions, she lived on a treadmill of sheer labor. Compared to their easy road of acknowledged great literary figures, her life path was a granite cliff sown with cactus and barbed wire.

But she had the immense daylight sense of reality they both lacked and, beyond that, something that Gide tried all his life to have, or to appear to have, and which he lacked to the end: a genuine moral sense founded on a genuine capacity for human feeling. She never attempts to haul God into criminal collusion with the spiritual deformities of her characters. Being a generous woman born to be exploited by men, she has for some of them the abject tenderness and indulgence which is so terribly womanly. Yet she knows this; she does not deceive herself. And her women, if possible less attractive even than the men, are still women, which Proust's never were.

The beings who people these six short novels are all of the race of the half-born, the incomplete, turning each one in his narrow space. They have no minds to speak of, they are in a limbo of physical indulgences, and they live and die their desolate lives in the longest waking dream. In the end, it is middle-classness, incapacity for tragedy—or comedy either—for faith, for any steadfastness except in delusion and obsession. It is stupidity—which the introduction once charitably tries to interpret as innocence.

The two must not be confounded, ever; innocence is a not-knowing of childhood, or inexperience. Stupidity is the inability to learn in spite of experience. Innocence can lead the innocent into evil; stupidity is itself an evil. Colette is the wisest kind of artist; the light of her quick intelligence plays over this Limbo, in her warmth of emotion she cannot reject or condemn them, and here is the strangest thing—the stories are full of light, and air, and greenery and freshness, the gayest sparkle of laughter, all in a way misleading, if you like; for there is a satire of the sharpest kind in this contrast between the sordidness, the obstinate dreariness, of human conduct and motive, and the disregarded, the ignored, the unused possibilities for human happiness.

Colette conceals her aim, her end, in her method. Without setting her up in rivalry with her great jealous, dubious male colleagues and contemporaries, let us just be glad of such a good, sound, honest artist, a hard-working one; we could really do nicely with more "light writers" like her. The really light-weight ones weigh a ton beside her.

✍ Appendix

Book Reviews Included in *The Collected Essays and Occasional Writings*

"Quetzalcoatl." *New York Herald Tribune Books,* March 7, 1926, p. 1. Review of *The Plumed Serpent,* by D. H. Lawrence (New York: Alfred A. Knopf, 1926). Reprinted in *The Days Before* and *The Collected Essays and Occasional Writings.*

"La Conquistadora." *New York Herald Tribune Books,* April 11, 1926, pp. 3–4. Review of *The Rosalie Evans Letters from Mexico,* arranged with comment by Daisy Caden Pettus (Indianapolis: Bobbs-Merrill Company, 1926). Revised and reprinted in *The Days Before* and *The Collected Essays and Occasional Writings.*

"Everybody Is a Real One." *New York Herald Tribune Books,* January 16, 1927, pp. 1–2. Review of *The Making of Americans,* by Gertrude Stein (Paris: Three Mountain Press, 1925). Reprinted in "Gertrude Stein: Three Views," in *The Days Before* and *The Collected Essays and Occasional Writings.*

"Second Wind." *New York Herald Tribune Books,* September 23, 1928, p. 6. Review of *Useful Knowledge,* by Gertrude Stein (New York: Payson and Clarke, 1928). Reprinted in "Gertrude Stein: Three Views," in *The Days Before* and *The Collected Essays and Occasional Writings.*

"The Art of Katherine Mansfield." *Nation,* vol. 145, no. 17 (October 23, 1937), pp. 435–36. Review of *The Short Stories of Katherine Mansfield* (New York: Alfred A. Knopf, 1937). Reprinted in *The Days Before* and *The Collected Essays and Occasional Writings.*

"The Winged Skull." *Nation,* vol. 157, no. 3 (July 17, 1943), pp. 72–73. Review of *This Is Lorence: A Narrative of the Reverend Laurence Sterne,* by Lodwick Hartley (Chapel Hill: University of North Carolina Press, 1943). Reprinted in *The Collected Essays and Occasional Writings.*

"Pull Dick, Pull Devil." *Nation,* vol. 161, no. 15 (October 13, 1945), pp. 376–78. Review of *Saints and Strangers,* by George F. Willison (New York: Reynal and Hitchcock, 1945). Reprinted in *The Collected Essays and Occasional Writings.*

"The Calm, Pure Art of Willa Cather," *New York Times Book Review,* September 25, 1949, p. 1. Review of *Willa Cather on Writing,* by Willa

Cather (New York: Alfred A. Knopf, 1949). Reprinted as "Reflections on Willa Cather" in *The Days Before* and *The Collected Essays and Occasional Writings.*

"Edith Sitwell's Steady Growth to Great Poetic Art." *New York Herald Tribune Book Review,* December 18, 1949, p. 1. Review of *The Canticle of the Rose, 1917–1949,* by Edith Sitwell (New York: Vanguard Press, 1949). Reprinted as "The Laughing Heat of the Sun" in *The Days Before* and *The Collected Essays and Occasional Writings.*

"Orpheus in Purgatory." *New York Times Book Review,* January 1, 1950, pp. 3, 10. Review of *Rilke and Benevenuta,* by M. von Hattenberg (New York: W. W. Norton and Company, 1949). Revised and reprinted in *The Days Before* and *The Collected Essays and Occasional Writings.*

"Virginia Woolf's Essays—A Great Art, a Sober Craft." *New York Times Book Review,* May 7, 1950, p. 3. Review of *The Captain's Death Bed and Other Essays,* by Virginia Woolf (New York: Harcourt, Brace and Company, 1950). Reprinted as "Virginia Woolf" in *The Days Before* and *The Collected Essays and Occasional Writings.*

"Beerbohm Bailiwick." *New York Times Book Review,* October 22, 1950, p. 5. Review of *And Even Now,* by Max Beerbohm (New York: E. P. Dutton and Company, 1950). Reprinted as "Max Beerbohm" in *The Days Before* and *The Collected Essays and Occasional Writings.*

"Yours, Ezra Pound." *New York Times Book Review,* October 29, 1950, pp. 4, 26. Review of *The Letters of Ezra Pound, 1907–1941,* ed. D. D. Paige (New York: Harcourt, Brace and Company, 1950). Revised and reprinted as " 'It Is Hard to Stand in the Middle' " in *The Days Before* and *The Collected Essays and Occasional Writings.*

"E. M. Forster Speaks Out for the Things He Holds Dear." *New York Times Book Review,* November 4, 1951, p. 3. Review of *Two Cheers for Democracy,* by E. M. Forster (New York: Harcourt, Brace and Company, 1951). Reprinted as "E. M. Forster" in *The Days Before* and *The Collected Essays and Occasional Writings.*

"On Christopher Sykes" (1950). *The Collected Essays and Occasional Writings* (New York: Delacorte Press, 1970), pp. 64–67. Review of *Character and Situation,* by Christopher Sykes, with an introduction by Evelyn Waugh (New York: Alfred A. Knopf, 1950).

"The Grand and the Tragic." *New York Times Book Review,* April 13, 1952, p. 3. Review of *Rome and a Villa,* by Eleanor Clark (New York: Doubleday and Company, 1952). Reprinted as "Eleanor Clark" in *The Collected Essays and Occasional Writings.*

"His Poetry Makes the Difference." *New York Times Book Review,* November 20, 1955, p. 5. Review of *Dylan Thomas in America,* by John

Malcolm Brinnin (Boston: Atlantic/Little, Brown, 1955). Reprinted in "Dylan Thomas" in *The Collected Essays and Occasional Writings.*

"In the Depths of Grief, a Towering Rage." *New York Times Book Review,* October 13, 1957, p. 3. Review of *Leftover Life to Kill,* by Caitlin Thomas (Boston: Atlantic/Little, Brown, 1957). Reprinted in "Dylan Thomas" in *The Collected Essays and Occasional Writings.*

"In the Morning of the Poet." *New York Times Book Review,* February 2, 1958, p. 4. Review of *Dylan Thomas: Letters to Vernon Watkins,* edited by Vernon Watkins (New York: New Directions, 1957). Reprinted in "Dylan Thomas" in *The Collected Essays and Occasional Writings.*

✍ Index